WEALTH & ASSET
PROTECTION STRATEGIES

A Simple and Effective
Guide To Keeping Everything You've Earned

By Steven Sears

EQUINET PUBLISHING

A

WEALTH & ASSET PROTECTION STRATEGIES

Printed in the United States of America

Library of Congress information is available from the publisher.

ISBN 0-929765-96-6

Published by Equinet Publishing

B

DEDICATION

I wish to give special thanks to my family, friends, employees and associates for their generous assistance without whom this book would not have been possible.

DISCLAIMER

Neither the publisher nor the author are rendering legal, tax, accounting, or other professional advice. Wealth preservation, estate planning, tax strategies and techniques depend upon an individual's facts and circumstances; accordingly, the information and opinions presented in this book must be correlated with the individual's situation to establish applicability. Moreover, because of the complexities of laws, the constant changes resulting from new developments, and the necessity of determining appropriateness to a particular individual, it is important that professional advice be sought before implementing the ideas suggested in this book.

Table of Contents

Dedication
About the author
Introduction

Chapter One   1
Estate Planning-*Protecting your family*
Goals
    Tools
    Revocable living trusts
    Pour over wills
    Durable powers of attorney
    Life insurance trusts
    Children's trusts
    Review

Chapter Two   14
Domestic asset protection-*Protecting your wealth*
Goals
    Tools
    Limited partnerships
    Limited Liability Companies
    Corporations
    Business structure
    Review

Chapter Three   33
Offshore asset protection-*Impenetrable structure*
Goals
    Tools
    Offshore banking
    Foreign companies
    International trusts
    Review

Chapter Four   56
Timing and planning-*Getting started*

Chapter Five   60
Other strategies-*Keeping it all*
    Marital agreements
    Tax collections
    Bankruptcy
    Retirement plans
    Collateralization & encumbrances

Conclusion

Appendix
    Selected domestic jurisdictions
    Selected offshore jurisdictions

About The Author

Steven Sears is a licensed Attorney, a Certified Public Accountant and an investment advisor with a Masters degree in Taxation. He has a Bachelor's degree in Business Administration and he is a licensed Real Estate Broker and a Law Professor.

He is the principal of Steven Sears—A Professional Corporation. Mr. Sears has been the featured speaker at hundreds of seminars and has been interviewed countless times on television and radio.

Mr. Sears' firm has offered personal service in the tax, legal, accounting, financial and international arenas since 1979.

His staff includes licensed professionals such as CPAs, attorneys, enrolled agents, investment advisors and a highly qualified support staff. In the area of asset protection and estate planning, his firm specializes in the formation and administration of business structures and holding companies. Through affiliated offices worldwide he maintains relationships with the largest and most reputable trust companies and banking institutions.

In addition, his firm can form offshore companies in almost any jurisdiction. Domestic planning includes formation of entities in all states including corporations, limited partnerships, limited liability companies and trusts.

For private banking and portfolio management, his firm has established relationships with many of the largest international banks around the world. They can also assist with management services that provide secrecy and confidentiality for your investments.

D

In the area of accounting and tax planning, the firm offers accounting services, preparation of financial statements, reviews, audits and general business consulting. Tax planning services are available for individuals, corporations, partnerships, estates, trusts and non-profit entities.

In other areas, the firm provides full legal representation in all matters including estate planning, bankruptcy, litigation, real estate, trademarks, contracts, general business and international law.

E

Introduction

I would like to ask you three simple questions. Is your net worth more than $100,000? More than likely your answer was yes. If you take a moment and think about it, you are probably worth more than that just because of the equity in your home. If you add in savings, stocks, bonds, insurance, home furnishings and the like, your net worth is probably much more than you realized.

Do you want to keep all these assets? Of course you do, but more than likely you haven't given much thought lately to the possibility that you might lose everything you own. After all, you have homeowner's, life, car, business and health insurance and a savings account that's federally insured as well. Your investment portfolio is probably well diversified and relatively stable and your home equity isn't going anywhere but up. So what's to worry about?

For starters, did you know that the estate tax now goes up to 50%? If you have more than $1,000,000 in net worth and you have not planned for your wealth and assets to be safely passed along to your heirs— the result is quite simple, the government is going to tax all of it including your business, home, savings and all your investments at this astounding rate.

Let's do some quick math. Let's say you have $300,000 in equity in your home. You also have an investment portfolio that is worth $400,000. You have a life insurance policy that's worth $700,000 to your beneficiaries or designates and your business is worth $500,000 net. That's a total of $1.9 million.

F

At the current estate tax rates, your heirs would have to pay over $400,000 in taxes! Where is your family going to get that money? Most likely they will have to sell your business and home and cash in most of your investments.

The Internal Revenue Service is just the tip of the iceberg though in terms of threats to your wealth and assets. What would happen if you were suddenly debilitated, certainly not a pleasant thought, but a realistic possibility. If you could no longer work or manage your own affairs, what good would a life insurance policy do you? Perhaps your health insurance would cover some of your bills, but what about the rest of your life and your family?

What if you are sued? Suppose one of your employees is involved in a costly auto accident while making deliveries for your company and the other party decided to sue you for more than your insurance covered. Suppose that employee of yours was *responsible* for that terrible accident and further suppose, you lost the case. You would want your assets protected wouldn't you? Judgment creditors can be extremely tenacious about seizing assets.

And suppose, like many other Americans the IRS suddenly seized your property and assets, what would you do? In one year alone recently, the IRS received nearly 10,000 taxpayer complaints over abusive collection practices. In addition, through the years, the IRS has seized tens of thousands of dollars worth of taxpayers' property including vehicles, homes and other real estate and levied hundreds of thousands of dollars worth of liens on people's property.

G

You may have heard this story, but it bears repeating. Back in the thirties there was a man by the name of Willie Sutton who was a prolific bank robber. When he was finally apprehended and asked by a newspaper reporter why he robbed banks, his reply was, "Because that's where the money is." A funny and appropriate story. Do you want your assets sitting in a bank in your name for the entire world to clearly see and gain access to? Do you want your real estate and other property titled in your name clearly visible for anyone to seize? Do you want your stocks and other investments to be so easily traceable? I think not. The point is quite clear, there are *many important reasons* to protect your wealth and assets.

Assuming you have already given asset protection some thought, you probably know that there have already been some books written on the subject, so you might be asking, do we really need another? My answer is, most definitely. After having given hundreds of seminars on this subject and helping thousands of individuals and businesses protect their assets and wealth. So many people asked me to write a book on the subject that I decided to take a look at what was already on the shelves. To my surprise the books that were available were mostly technical and not one of them was even remotely understandable to the average person.

I am an attorney, a CPA and I hold a Masters degree in taxation and I have found that most people cannot understand the complex legal issues which are discussed in most of the books currently out on the subject. I'm sure that they contain viable and even helpful information, but most of them are filled

H

with too many complex charts, tons of "legalese" and other unimportant and confusing information.

In short, I decided what was needed was a simple, easy-to-read guide that the average person could understand and use effectively to protect their assets and wealth.

Wealth and Asset Protection Strategies is the result of this effort and this is my promise to you:

You will learn why and how you can protect your personal and business assets and wealth from lawsuits, the Internal Revenue Service, collection agencies, inflation and the decrease in asset values. You will also learn why and how you should protect your estate for your heirs. In addition, you will learn why and how you can protect your privacy and literally become anonymous. And last, you will learn all of this quickly and painlessly–you may even be entertained a little.

One final word before we begin. This is not a book for alarmists, cultists, money launderers, drug dealers, or even those who are just plain paranoid. It is for the prudent, intelligent, average person who has worked hard to earn a good living; has acquired a certain amount of wealth and assets and who wants to insure, beyond a shadow of a doubt, that his or her assets and family are fully protected. It is also for those who like to enjoy a good night's sleep.

Chapter One
Estate planning
Protecting your family

I am going to describe all of the methods that you have at your disposal to protect yourself, your assets and your wealth. All of these methods or tools, as I refer to them, are not only legal and ethical, they are *essential* to protecting and preserving what is yours.

Think of these techniques as building blocks. You can either build a short wall just to keep prying eyes off of you and your assets or you can use these building blocks to construct an impenetrable fortress around you, your family, your business and your assets—a fortress so strong and tall that no one will ever know who lives in it or what it contains. Now that's privacy!

You can use a few building blocks, or you can use as many as your circumstances warrant, it's strictly up to you and your own particular needs. These building blocks fall into five categories. They include **Estate Planning, Asset Protection, Offshore Asset Protection, Timing and Planning and Additional Strategies.**

The beginning building blocks

There are a wealth of tools and strategies contained within each of these categories from which you can choose to protect all of your assets and wealth including: Living Trusts, Insurance Trusts, Children's Trusts, Corporations and Limited Liability Companies.

Think of it this way, if you lose all of your assets and wealth to the IRS, a lawsuit, a debilitating disease, injury, divorce, bankruptcy or creditors, it will only be because of one reason—you didn't plan ahead. It's just that simple. Asset protection is all about planning; planning well in advance of the time when you might need it.

The best time to implement one or all of these methods is when you are healthy, clear thinking and you still have your property, money, investments and possessions—not *after* trouble begins.

I promised you this would be simple so I am going to start with the most basic topic of all, Estate Planning. This is the first building block for anyone with significant assets.

Estate Planning Goals

1. Insuring that your wealth and assets go quickly to your heirs upon your death
2. Minimize the erosion of your estate by estate taxes
3. Eliminate probate hassles and expenses.

Tools

1. Revocable Living Trusts
2. Pour Over Wills
3. Durable Powers of Attorney
4. Life Insurance Trusts
5. Children's Trusts

You would be surprised at the number of people who don't have a Will, but what is even more remarkable is how many people *have* a Will and *think* that it protects and preserves their assets and wealth for their heirs.

First of all, if you don't have a Will, everything you own may ultimately go to the wrong individual or individuals and/or the government. In any case, those left behind will find themselves in a quagmire of legal hassles at best, that could go on for years and years. And at worst, your heirs could forfeit most of whatever you left behind.

Even if you do have a Will and you have carefully designated all the beneficiaries and what they are to receive, your heirs will still have to go through a lengthy and costly probate process in court that could last many years. In addition, anything over the current amount that is exempted from taxes can be taxed at over 50%. Besides, a probated Will is a public document, it is available through public records for anyone and everyone to read. Do you really want the world to know what you have left to your family? There is a better way, a much better way, it's called a Living Trust.

Tools
Revocable Living Trusts

A Revocable Living Trust is quite simply a document that acts like a very private and secure box into which you place your assets and wealth. It is a document that is not available to public eyes because it is not part of any public record.

With a Living Trust, you are in complete control of all your assets. You can be the sole trustee or there can be more than one trustee such as you and your spouse. You designate who your beneficiaries are, what they will receive and how they will receive it. For example, if you are very wealthy and you have young children, you may not want them to have all of your assets and wealth at once. You could stagger the distribution of your wealth over a long period of time. For example, you may feel it more prudent to let them have some percentage of it only after they have finished college and then perhaps some more when they reach the age of 35 and yet more later on. It's up to you, you are completely in control.

You can also designate another trustee to take immediate control of your trust upon your death, eliminating the need for probate and any other court involvement.

With only a Will, if you were to become mentally incapacitated, you would no longer have the power to conduct your own affairs. At that point a court could step in and take over and once that happens they usually stay in control until you recover or die. With a Living Trust that won't happen. You will have already appointed someone you trust to take immediate control as the new trustee in your mental or physical "absence."

Since all of your assets are now contained within the trust and are titled in the name of the trust—not in your name—you personally own nothing (do not have title to anything that would be subject to probate upon your death). However, during your lifetime, you would still completely control your assets as the trustee.

Additionally, we can insert a "no-contest" clause into your trust. This means that disgruntled or disinherited heirs who may have been included, would now be excluded from any distributions if they ever challenged the trust through a lawsuit or other means.

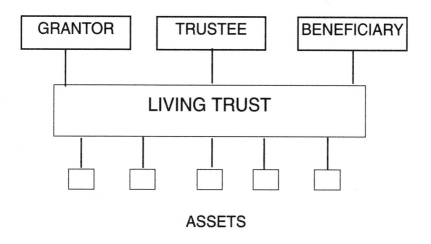

With respect to estate taxes, the current exemption is soon expected to rise to $1,000,000 or more with tax rates up to approximately 50% of the value of your estate. However, if you are married you can create what is known as an "A-B" Trust. This gives both you and your spouse a $1 million exemption each, allowing you to pass along over $2 million to your heirs.

A more sophisticated strategy involves an A-B-C trust where the C trust can go to the children from prior marriages and where you can still have various "strings attached" to later distributions.

For wealthier individuals you can even structure generation skipping transfers, effectively moving assets to grandchildren while avoiding additional estates taxes, as those assets pass through to younger generations.

Another interesting feature of the Revocable Living Trust is that you can name the trust as you wish. I always recommend a generic name like the "Seawind Trust" or the "Capital Investment Trust" or any generic name you feel comfortable with. I prefer this type of name rather than the "John and Susan Smith Family Trust," for the obvious reason of added privacy.

When you open bank accounts and transfer real estate this name goes on the title of any assets which you own. By using an independent trustee and a generic name for the trust, you can actually achieve a great deal of privacy. Remember that the trust is still a private document as well, and is not available for the public to read.

Transferring your current assets into a Living Trust is relatively easy with the changing of titles taking only a short time.

Tools
Pour Over Will

Keep in mind, you would still have a Will when you form a trust only now, you would use what we call a "Pour Over Will." This takes the assets through the Will and pours them over into the living trust. Assets like furniture, artwork, jewelry; things that don't normally carry a title, would go into the Pour Over Will. By assigning these assets to the Living Trust or having the Pour Over Will pick them up, we have an organized method of distributing assets to heirs while avoiding probate.

With the Will you can also designate a guardian for your children in the event of your death. This would ensure that the proper person or persons in your family would take care of your child or children in your absence. This way you can pre-designate a person who has the skill, knowledge and compassion to care for your loved ones in times of need. You can just imagine how few people could step into such a special position.

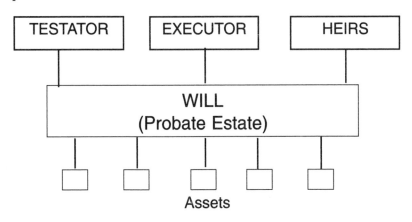

Durable Powers of Attorney
Asset management

A Durable Power of Attorney is a document designating an individual, which can be a family member or friend, to manage your assets or your healthcare needs in your absence. Should you become incapacitated physically and/or mentally (one or two physicians would have to certify this), then the individual you have chosen would automatically be able to manage your assets until such time as you were able to do this yourself once again.

You should choose someone with particular financial skills, someone who can prudently and conservatively handle your property and investments on your behalf and for your family and future heirs. This can involve taking care of rental properties or even paying the mortgage and bills for your current home. This is a much better alternative to a conservatorship where a court appointed representative ends up managing all your assets.

Healthcare Needs

If you became ill, had a stroke or were in a situation where you might be subjected to being put on a life support system, a Durable Power of Attorney for Health Care would designate an individual to handle your health-care needs.

Suppose you did not want to be put on a life support system or to remain in a vegetative state the rest of your life, the individual you have designated to handle these situations is empowered through the Durable Powers of Attorney to ensure that your wishes are carried out. Likewise, any other wishes you had about any and all treatments such as surgery, would be carried out for you as well as your wishes after your death including such things as autopsies, burials, cremations and the like.

In these situations, where very difficult and serious decisions must be made, you may not be able to communicate with your physician or your family, due to your medical, physical or mental state. However, they can refer to this document to get an understanding of your real intent, whatever it may be.

And now, when all is well and everyone is healthy, is the best time to memorialize these decisions, not when you are in a dire emergency and unable to make these decisions.

Tools
Life Insurance Trusts

Many people do not realize that the value of their life insurance upon their death becomes a taxable event. Let's say you have property, cash and investments worth $2 million and you also have a life insurance policy that will pay your children $1 million upon your death. That $1 million will be included when the Internal Revenue Service is calculating the amount of your estate taxes; that is, if you just leave a Will and/or you don't plan for that eventuality now.

If you had an "A-B" Living Trust, your exemption would be over $2 million but that would still leave you with the $1 million life insurance policy pay out, which would be taxable.

There is a way to avoid all of this pain and it's called a Life Insurance Trust. Your insurance policy becomes an asset of your trust and the premium to be paid upon your death would be designated as "gifts." Since you are allowed to give gifts of up to $10,000 per year non-taxable to whomever you wish, the premiums would be divided up in lots of $10,000 gifts each year for each of your children and your spouse, or whomever you designate, thus taking it completely out of your estate. A trustee is assigned to this trust just like in a Revocable Living Trust.

Upon your death the proceeds of the life insurance would then go tax free to your children and you could also provide for your spouse and other family members as well.

Tools
Children's trusts

A Children's Trust can be set up to gift part of your estate to future generations. This can be done while still maintaining some control over how your children will be able to spend that money.

Just imagine what an eighteen-year old would do if he or she got a few hundred thousand dollars all at one time? I would think a sports car, vacation, new clothes and a few friends might help them go through it quite quickly.

It is better that you designate a proper trustee to handle that wealth, perhaps for college, health care and basic support. Then at a more prudent age, say twenty-five or thirty, or upon marriage, all of the proceeds could be distributed. This way you can avoid having these funds disappear or have them fall into the wrong hands. Also remember that each child or individual can receive up to $10,000 per year free of taxes. If you are married, this amount doubles to $20,000 per year.

One example of the importance of a Children's Trust involved the true case of a family which was comprised of a father that was 35, a mother that was 29 and 2 children ages 3 and 5 with another child on the way.

As a regular client, we emphasized to the father and mother the important need for estate planning. However, tragedy struck before this plan was set into motion. Unfortunately, the birth of their third child became complicated. The mother died but the child survived, all of the mother's insurance policy proceeds were designated to the children as beneficiaries. Therefore, all of the proceeds of the $1 million dollar policy were blocked from disbursement until each child reached the age of 18.

Unfortunately, the father had very limited resources and could not provide for the family alone so the insurance policy was of no help to him.

Had he set up the trust prior to the mother's death, the funds from the insurance policy would have been available to help the father raise his family.

Review
Revocable Living Trusts
Benefits

1. Private not public
2. All assets owned by and titled in the trust, not in your name
3. Upon death, no lengthy and expensive probate
4. Can reduce or eliminate estate taxes
5. Can have one trustee or several
6. Can designate all beneficiaries and determine distribution of assets
7. Allows quick distribution of assets to beneficiaries
8. Upon becoming incapacitated, can use Durable Powers of Attorney to assign someone to manage your assets and an individual to manage your health care needs.
9. Can be changed or revoked
10. Relatively easy to do
11. Keeps disgruntled and disinherited heirs away from your assets
12. Can assign a guardian for your children through your Will.

Life Insurance Trust
Benefits

1. Reduces estate taxes
2. Controls the pay out to beneficiaries
3. Use an independent trustee
4. Provides for spouse and children

Children's Trusts
Benefits

1. Reduces estate taxes
2. Can gift $10,000 per year, per parent, tax-free
3. Can dictate how much and when children receive assets

Chapter Two
Domestic Asset Protection
Protecting your wealth

Goals

1. Use of one or more entities to protect businesses and personal assets from creditors, judgments and seizures.
2. Minimize federal and state taxes.
3. Confidential ownership of business and personal assets

Tools

1. Limited partnerships
2. Limited liability companies
3. Corporations

Our next set of building blocks would include the methods and vehicles available to you to protect *all* of your assets and wealth. This would include personal and business protection from the IRS, lawsuits, creditors, accidents and divorce proceedings.

This is the section where we start to build your impenetrable fortress. There are many different ways to protect your assets. These would include Limited Partnerships, Limited Liability Companies and various forms of Corporations.

Tools
Limited partnerships

A limited partnership is comprised of one General Partner and one or more Limited Partners. The General Partner is the only one who controls the partnership, its assets and its wealth. Now remember, assets are anything with value; this can be real estate, investments, cash and even art, cars, boats and airplanes.

Like a Living Trust, a Limited Partnership is nothing more than a document or an entity, which legally holds title to assets. In a Limited Partnership, you would obviously make yourself the General Partner or the Managing Partner. You can have as many Limited Partners as you like but none of them exert any control over the partnership or its assets. You can be the only person who has put any assets into the partnership, or your Limited Partners can also put assets into the partnership, thus giving title of those assets to the partnership and not to themselves.

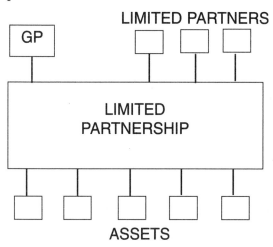

You could put as little as $1,000 of actual cash into starting the partnership. All other assets such as real estate, cars, boats, art, stocks, bonds; anything and everything of value would be owned by the Limited Partnership—not you.

As an example, you could make your two children your Limited Partners giving each of them 1% ownership in the partnership. You and your wife could own the other 98%. Obviously the percentages would change depending upon the number of children you have. Then you could conceivably give each of your children a gift of $20,000 tax-free each year ($10,000 by each parent) by placing this amount, as an asset into the partnership.

If you didn't want them to take possession of that money for whatever reason, they could not withdraw it, because you are the controlling partner. You are the only one with voting rights. You have given them an intangible asset, namely an interest in a Limited Partnership, but the assets remain in the name of the partnership.

We call this a "strings attached gift." Of course, you love your children, so you would want to provide for them but you wouldn't want to give up control during your lifetime. Children go through divorces, lawsuits, business break ups and the like, so sometimes it is more prudent to treat gifts in this manner.

Say for instance, a child turns 21 and they want to spend this money that you have been gifting them for years (which has also been growing through appreciation as well). They can't spend this money unless you change the partnership. They can't sell the assets because nobody wants to buy a minimal interest in a family Limited Partnership. They can't demand any distributions because the assets are owned by the partnership and controlled by you. Essentially, until you decide to distribute this money to them, it's nothing more than a piece of paper; an intangible ownership.

The children cannot sell it, encumber it, gift it or transfer it to a spouse; you maintain complete control. I call it "having your cake and eating it too." You have gifted it to your children and have still maintained control and you have protected it from lawsuits.

Furthermore, upon starting a Limited Partnership, you can make your Revocable Living Trust an asset of this new Partnership.

The Limited Partnership also provides an excellent vehicle to hold your investment portfolio. Your stocks, bonds, mutual funds and other liquid investments can be held within the Limited Partnership by having your brokerage account titled in the partnership name. For example, "Capital Ventures LP." This gives you, as General Partner, complete trading authority and control of the banking through your signature on the account. You can even trade on-line using your password or code. Of course, your statements now are in the name of the partnership, further protecting your privacy.

You have now effectively put a few more rows of blocks on top of your fortress walls, further insulating you and your assets from everyone and everything.

Limited Liability Companies

A Limited Liability Company (LLC) is another vehicle for protecting your assets and is more sophisticated than a Limited Partnership. In comparing an LLC to a Limited Partnership there are two distinct differences. In a Limited Partnership, the limited partners cannot participate in managing the business, in an LLC they can. In a Limited Partnership the general partners are personally liable for business debts, in an LLC, all owners get the benefit of limited liability protection from business debts and claims.

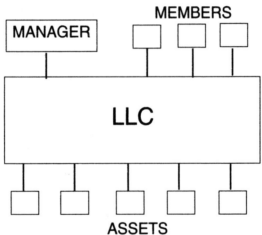

Limited Liability Companies were first created in Europe. These were hybrids that utilized the best attributes of a corporation and a partnership. The best attribute of a partnership is that it is "tax neutral." In other words, the tax effect flows through it to the individual so it's taxed like a sole proprietorship.

The downside of the typical partnership however is "liability." When you are a General Partner, you are fully exposed to liabilities, not only for your own acts, but also for those of your partners. A general partnership can be formed very easily; even a verbal agreement or just a handshake can create a partnership. If a partner signs a contract, you are liable for the terms of that contract.

In order to eliminate this downside of the partnership, we create an entity similar to a limited partnership, a merger of the best of a corporation and a limited partnership. This is the "Limited Liability Company." This type of entity has a manager or managers, which would be you or whomever you wish and as many additional members as you wish. Each of these members can contribute assets to the LLC.

The manager does just that, he manages or controls all the assets. Neither the manager nor the members have any personal liability for debts of the entity, they're merely investors.

LLCs are excellent vehicles for holding liquid assets as well as business, investment and real estate assets. Wyoming was the first state to permit LLCs and now 49 states have LLC statutes. Now that LLCs have been around many years, people are very comfortable with them. You actually now see many companies and professionals operating as LLCs, or LLPs (a similar form for licensed professionals). Even the IRS has fully approved their use and tax effects.

Now, let's talk about the asset protection attributes of an LLC. In an LLC, if one of the members is involved in an accident, is sued for any reason, or goes through a divorce the only consequence to the LLC and yourself is that any judgment that may be exacted against that member can not be a judgment against the LLC. The creditor or judgment holder is only going to go after that partner's personal assets, which of course, have already been titled to the LLC.

All that person owns is a portion of an LLC, and, of course, the manager is not going to distribute any funds or assets to that partner who may have a judgment against him or her.

What a creditor or judgment holder would get, if they prevailed in a lawsuit, would be a "Charging Order." This means they could charge against any income that comes to the individual to which they have obtained a judgment. But since the manager isn't going to distribute any income or assets to that partner, the creditor gets nothing. Meanwhile, because the tax effects still flow through to that individual via the K-1 form, with no income to pay the tax liability, the tax liability can actually flow through to the creditor, instead of your partner.

Can you imagine being a creditor with nothing but a huge tax liability from a K-1 to show for all your collection attempts? This can quickly encourage a creditor to settle the judgment for a mere fraction of the total amount. Our firm has been successful in settling such cases for pennies on the dollar. Just imagine being a judgment creditor and having to wait years to collect your judgment. Remember how accounts receivable psychology works. After 30, 60 or 90 days of going unpaid, their value diminishes. After several years of being uncollectible, that judgment is virtually worthless. Add to this, the potential for the creditor to be saddled with his debtor's taxes and you can begin to see how attractive this type of set up can be to those who want to protect their assets.

If there is a judgement, I recommend waiting a few years and then offering the plaintiff a small settlement, say $1,000 or $10,000 on a $100,000 or more judgment. Actually by this time, the plaintiff's attorney who sued you and who probably worked on a contingency arrangement, would love to get any reasonable amount, if you *did* want to settle the case.

If the plaintiff is still not interested in pursuing a collection we can always threaten bankruptcy if necessary, but usually the mere threat of that will encourage a settlement.

Nevada, Delaware and Wyoming are excellent jurisdictions for LLCs because these states have no state taxes and these jurisdictions guard the privacy of corporations more closely than other states. Also, they are not as cooperative with the IRS as are some other jurisdictions and filing fees are very low.

Let's talk about the privacy aspects of LLCs. First you choose a generic name for your LLC like Equity Holdings, LLC. Now, your name will not show up on the title of any asset including real estate, bank accounts and even your home. If someone was to try to determine if you owned the home you were living in, it would appear as though you were renting the property because a title search would reveal that the property was owned by Equities Holding LLC, or whatever name you choose for your company. Actually, to make your LLC bullet proof we can make you a tenant and actually have you pay rent to your own LLC. This strategy is best when a creditor is lurking at your doorstep and you really need the protection. We than take those rent payments that you make to the LLC and use them to pay any mortgage or expenses to maintain the property. In any case, the property and the funds are well protected.Think about it, once someone knows you own a particular piece of property it only takes about ten minutes to obtain a property profile from public records and determine: who is on title, the market value, how much equity is in the home, if there is a 2nd or 3rd mortgage, who has liens on the property and more! *You* can actually obtain this record on anyone including your own neighbors.

So far, using our beginning building blocks, we have achieved maximized estate planning exclusions, asset protection and total anonymity and privacy.

The tax effects of an LLC are important as well. LLCs are taxed as partnerships flowing the tax attribute directly to the members. We can actually control this taxing method by using a "Check The Box" rule. This means you can choose to file as a corporation or a partnership simply by checking the appropriate box on the tax forms.

Also, LLCs offer much more flexibility when dealing with tax regulators. LLCs do not have many of the limitations of S-corporations, such as limits on the number of shareholders and classes of stock. Also, foreign individuals, foreign companies, trusts and other corporations can be members of an LLC.

Another tax benefit of LLCs or for that matter, partnerships, is that you can specifically allocate income and expenses to various members of the LLC. That means that taxable income could be allocated to children or family members in lower tax brackets and deductions or losses could be allocated to the members with the highest tax brackets, thus saving the family taxes as a whole.

Tools
Corporations

We have talked quite a bit about *personal* assets, so now let's address your *business* assets. So many people these days are enjoying the booming economy through the rapid growth of their businesses and its assets. Either people have, or are going to, start a small business as a sole proprietorship, partnership or a corporation. Keep in mind that LLCs can be used for small businesses or investments but corporations are better entities for operating an *active business*.

Sole proprietorships are out of the question except for the simplest business because all of the liability rests with you, the owner. So your next step might be to "incorporate" your business. At this point in our discussions you have limited your personal liability. Now this new corporation or company has its own, separate legal existence. When you execute a contract you would only sign in the name of the corporation. Remember to always sign the name of the corporation, then your name followed by, Vice President, etc., not your own name. This insures that liabilities always rest with the corporation.

Assets would be owned in the name of the corporation. Debts, including credit cards, vehicle loans, mortgages and the like would be in the corporate name. You would also want to avoid signing any "personal" guarantees. This can expose you to liability if the corporation cannot pay the debts it incurs. Often many lenders will lend without it. And you can always limit any guarantees to small amounts.

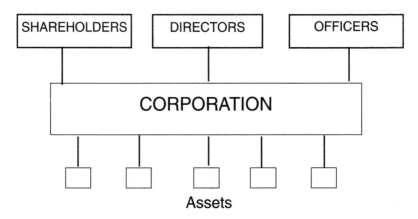
Assets

Through the corporation you have limited your liability and gained a great deal of privacy and protection. Perhaps you start your corporation with as little as a $1,000 investment and that initial capital would be the limit of your exposure to any lawsuits or judgments. Thus your first level of protection for your small business is to incorporate. A corporation offers many tax benefits, unlike a sole proprietorship. By using a corporation, you can take advantage of the 15% tax bracket which is a lot lower than individual rates, which can go all the way up to 39%, and that doesn't include the state's share.

In addition, small businesses have always been a favorite of Congress. As a small corporation you can get what is called a Section 179 deduction. This is a deduction from your taxes for all the business equipment that you buy during the year. Typically you can write off up to about $20,000 worth of equipment. Without this immediate write off, you could be stuck with a depreciation schedule that would spread out your deductions over several years instead of enjoying all of it in one year.

Another benefit of becoming a corporation is the judicious use of the "fiscal" year. As an individual or sole proprietor, your year begins like everyone else's, on January 1 and runs through December 31, but once you form a corporation, you can designate whatever date you wish as your fiscal year end. It could be any month in the year; whatever is most beneficial to you.

The benefit is this—suppose you have had a great deal of income this past year as a sole proprietor and your tax liabilities are going to be enormous. Perhaps you have also had a lot of profits, but no cash at the moment because you have reinvested the profits of your small business back into the business. Where are you going to get the money to pay the taxes? It's all tied up in receivables and/or new equipment or whatever. Your profit is sitting there on paper, but it isn't in your bank account.

In this instance, as a new corporation, you would choose to stagger your calendar year. So for example, you could now change your fiscal year end to June 30, effectively giving yourself another six months of breathing room before you had to file your taxes.

Furthermore, let's say you have a large profit of $300,000 this year and you want to pay yourself a bonus. You could pay this bonus on January 3rd as opposed to

December 31st, effectively moving this income into the next year and moving the date you have to pay taxes out on it a year further. Other benefits of corporations are that pension plans are more generous and health insurance plans, vehicle reimbursement plans, expense accounts and employee benefit programs are easy to set up. These offer greater tax breaks than through sole proprietorships or partnerships.

In addition, when you're an officer of a small corporation, everything paid through the corporation is presumed to be a business expense for the most part. So, as an officer you can have an expense account which would include credit cards in the corporate name for travel, entertainment, marketing and to purchase supplies and pay car expenses, etc.

As a sole proprietor the IRS would scrutinize these types of deductions much more thoroughly than they would a corporation because these types of deductions are expected and are more a "normal course of business" for a corporation. Privacy is also another benefit of being incorporated. Shareholder's names are not a matter of public record. And if you use states like Nevada for your corporation, you can use "bearer stock" which is stock that is not held in a particular name. Stocks are issued to the bearer, which means whoever holds them, owns them, effectively insulating your privacy even further.

Imagine the added privacy you can achieve by merely handing the bearer stock to another person and thereby removing yourself as the owner. This technique could be very powerful prior to a debtor's examination or a deposition where a plaintiff is trying to discover your assets. Now you have effectively protected your assets and also your income.

As a corporation you are going to pay corporate taxes on your net business income. Additionally you will personally pay taxes on any money you have distributed to yourself through a salary or bonuses. And, of course, the more money the corporation makes, the larger and larger your tax liabilities grow.

If you haven't started your corporation yet, or even if you have, you may want to convert the corporation to either an LLC or turn it into an S- corporation. The standard corporation, within which you would have a corporate and individual tax liability, is called a "C" corporation. In a C-corporation, tax rates range from 15% up to $50,000 of profits, to 25% of the next $25,000. After this, the rates begin to get closer to individual rates, which are quite high.

So, what can we do about this? Your first thought might be to take the corporate profits for your small business and tax them at the corporate rates and retain them within the corporation or, take it out as a W2 wage or distribute it as a dividend. However, the problem with  dividends is double taxation—none of which is a good way to go.

Because of the tax situation of the C-Corporation, we

may now consider converting your small business to an S-corporation, which among other things can handle unlimited amounts of income distributions and can also deduct losses of the business at the individual level. Therefore, as an S-corporation, in terms of taxes, we are back to a "flow through" situation similar to a partnership.

Let's discuss S-corporations further. Only certain corporations can qualify as S-corporations. For one thing, you can not have any more than 75 shareholders. All shareholders must be U.S. citizens and the corporation can only have one class of stock. All shareholders must be individuals or estates or certain trusts. And the S-corporation cannot be a member of a group of affiliated corporations. However, an S-corporation can own other S-corporations, so they do offer many planning opportunities for multiple businesses.

Also, S-corporations can save you payroll taxes. Any flow-through dividends are not subject to social security and state payroll taxes. This way we can keep your W-2 wages relatively low and save you thousands of dollars.

As you can see, all of these entities that we have been discussing have their advantages and disadvantages depending upon your own particular needs. You will obviously want to carefully think over what type of entity you want your business to be, one that offers the most benefits to you.

Imagine this scenario: You are flying first class to Nevada to have your first corporate board meeting. Accommodations have been set up at the Bellagio Hotel for you and your board members to use one of the beautiful conference rooms in which to hold your meeting.

Of course your meeting would be catered with the finest appetizers and entrees you could imagine, complimented by a bottle of Dom Perignon. After your monthly board

meeting, you decide you want to travel by limousine to an elegant dinner and a spectacular show, after which you get extremely lucky and win thousands of dollars at the tables.

In the morning you sleep in and when you are ready, you go down to the pool and enjoy your own private cabana with a massage poolside while sipping pina coladas in the clean, warm, dry desert air. I don't know about you, but I would much rather conduct my corporate meetings in this manner than to sit in a stuffy conference room in a high rise building in downtown Los Angeles and then go home to leftovers for dinner.

Remember, all of this includes the fact that in many cases, all of this is a business expense and as such, can be a tax deduction charged to your Nevada corporation. Why not build up your business, enjoy life and at the same time have the added benefit of a tax saving?

Business Structure

There are a lot of situations where people own several businesses within one company; a chain of restaurants for example. When one of the restaurants experiences a problem, the entire chain is threatened. This could be due to financial difficulties or as the result of a lawsuit. Years ago we had a client who owned several locations of Mexican restaurants. As he got older and his business became more successful, he allowed his family members to manage each location; brothers, sisters, nieces, nephews. It turned out that one of the nephews did not have any particular talent as a manager and the restaurant subsequently became mired in debt as a result of this family member's mis-management.

This client's business structure lacked any formality, it was basically a massive sole proprietorship owned by our client. The client eventually had to file for Chapter 11 bankruptcy to gain the time to reorganize and attempt to pay off his creditors. He almost lost everything due to poor planning or rather, a lack of planning.

After getting him out of the mess we suggested the following; each restaurant location be its own corporation and

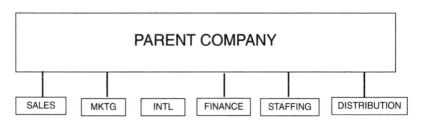

a parent or umbrella corporation be set up to order food and supplies for the entire group. Then, if one location went bad, at least he wouldn't lose them all. If one did have trouble it could could file for individual bankruptcy. In some cases we even designate divisions. For example, if yours is a manufacturing business, you may designate one entity as the manufacturing division and the other as the sales division. And if you do business on an international level, you could even have an international division, each division being a separate corporation to further minimize the risk of forfeiture of the overall corporate assets...."Just another brick on the wall," as the old Pink Floyd song goes. What this means is that the physical and tangible assets are held in one corporation however, the other divisions or corporations under the overall corporate umbrella, the ones that deal with the public and have a higher public profile, own no assets.

Let's review what we have accomplished so far. What kind of wall or fortress have we managed to build?

1. We have achieved the estate planning objectives of maximizing the exclusions upon death and not just up to $1,000,000. And all of the future appreciation can go to your beneficiaries as well.
2. We have also achieved asset protection, because the assets are all owned by the LLC including liquid, real estate securities, boats, cars, planes, and rental property.

3. We have also gained total anonymity. Remember that you can call your LLC anything you wish. And if you designate an independent trustee for your Living Trust, which is a member of your LLC, you hold all of the assets, but your name appears no where.

We have now added additional blocks to your fortress

Chapter Three
Offshore asset protection
Impenetrable structure
Goals

1. Secrecy/Privacy
2. Safety
3. Convenience
4. Tax structure

Tools

1. Private banking
2. Offshore companies
3. International trusts

Tools
Private Banking

Now we are going to discuss the most exciting and interesting aspect of asset protection. To this point we have built a lot of very high walls of protection around you, but we have not finished building your fortress.

The words, "offshore banking" usually elicit the same response in most people, "Too risky," but believe me, nothing could be further from the truth. In the United States we have a law called, The Bank Secrecy Act. Most American citizens feel that U.S. banks are quite safe, and they are. However, they aren't nearly as *secretive* as you would imagine. For one thing, you can get all the information you need about anyone's U.S. bank account just by knowing their 10 digit account number. Let's say someone has paid you or your business by check. You can find out how much is in that person's account just by calling their bank and telling them you have a check that is drawn on that bank account for "X" amount using the account number on the bottom of the check. Then you would ask the bank that if you were to deposit that check for X amount today, would it clear? The bank will tell you either, yes, or no. By calling several times, escalating the amount each time you call, you would eventually find the uppermost amount that would clear that account, thus knowing approximately how much is in it.

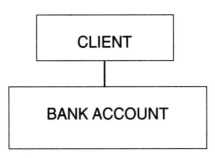

In addition, the new trend in U.S. banking has been the selling of customer information to telemarketing companies; another way banks earn money. In some cases, your name is given out, your account balances your social security number and more! *Now,* how secret do you think your bank is? Essentially, the Bank Secrecy Act means nothing.

Now, take the situation of offshore banks. First of all, it is estimated that more than two-thirds of all the world's wealth resides in offshore accounts! Offshore banks or banks in certain international jurisdictions, unlike U.S. banks, have very strong criminal laws concerning secrecy. In these international banks, if an employee gives out confidential information on an account, that employee and the bank can be held criminally liable.

Banking offshore is really not that unusual. Think of it this way; banks in the United States are "offshore" banks to those who live outside our borders. If a person from England opens an account in New York, he has an offshore account. Barclays Bank, in London, one of the oldest and largest banks in the world and one of the most powerful globally; certainly stronger than most U.S. banks, is an offshore bank to U.S. citizens.

Today, a great deal of your banking is done via the Internet. Calls to 800 numbers can be made to banks all the way across the continent. ATMs are located in other cities and states. So what is the difference in calling an 800 number or accessing an ATM for an account in Atlanta or in the Caribbean; both are in the same time zones?

Actually offshore banks are more like stock brokers or financial planners. In the U.S. generally speaking, banks and stock brokers are separate entities but in an offshore bank, these two entities are far more likely to be the same person. When you invest with an offshore bank you aren't just putting cash into a savings account; you can be investing in other assets such as stocks, bonds and other securities, just as you would here. To simplify matters, let's use this example. If you have a million dollars you wish to put into an offshore account, you could just deposit the money or you might want to buy a certain amount of shares of Microsoft, Coca-Cola, or U.S. Treasury Bonds; whatever suits your needs. This becomes your portfolio of assets.

Depending upon your near and long term needs you would obviously use a sensible asset allocation plan in which to hold these securities in your offshore account. So, what is the difference between calling your Merrill Lynch broker in Los

Angeles or your broker at your offshore bank in Europe? Your offshore bank and brokerage account is strictly secret, more so than any brokerage account in the U.S. and that's just one of the many differences.

However, just because you open your account with an offshore bank, that doesn't mean that the bank is necessarily going to manage your account, you can still manage your own account as you see fit, it's up to you. You are in complete control through the use of confidential passwords and pin codes.

Another misnomer is the fact that you must have millions of dollars to open an offshore account. The fact is you can open an offshore account with a nominal balance, in most cases $1,000 is sufficient. There are large banks like Barclays but there are many smaller ones that want your business as well. They can provide you with ATM cards, checking accounts, wire transfers, travelers checks and all the typical bank services that you already use here in the U.S.

In addition, all of the bank representatives that we have relationships with speak English and most of them send representatives to our offices several times a year to meet with our mutual clients.

With respect to the privacy of any communications that would require using the mail, those are handled in the strictest confidence as well. Anything that comes into the U.S. is hand delivered in an envelope addressed to our office. Your statement or whatever you have requested is then given to you personally in the privacy of our offices or re-mailed to you in a plain envelope. There are banks in Europe, The Caribbean, Asia and over 30 jurisdictions all over the world that are eager to have your account, large or small. In fact, most of the smaller nations *depend* upon banking as well as tourism for their very survival. They produce very little in the way of exportable products, so banking is an important industry and it's treated with the safety and dignity that importance implies. Like all of the other options in this book, offshore accounts can be simple and small or they can be more sophisticated and large. If you have a larger account, it is quite easy to set up online access via the Internet, just as you would here. You can go online 24 hours a day and visit your assets, access your balances and make ATM withdrawals here in the U.S. or just about anywhere else.

Take for example this true client scenario. Our client was a construction contractor who was responsible for many *sub-contractor's* bills. Several years ago he began to sense that the developer who hired him to work on a particularly large contract, might have been headed for potential money problems. Luckily he had already planned for such contingencies years before when he set up his asset protection plan with our firm.

Then one day, as fate would have it, the developer *did* file for bankruptcy leaving our client holding the bag for all of the other contractors he had hired. He ended up owing these sub contractors nearly $2 million and they, of course, wanted their money, so they initiated a plethora of lawsuits. However, all of his liquid assets had already been set up in an offshore trust earlier. He had nothing to worry about.

In fact, he was sick of the up and down cycles of real estate development anyway, so he took his yacht, which we had already registered in a Caribbean country, and he sailed all the way down the coast of Mexico, through the Panama Canal and into the Caribbean, where he and his wife now live on that same yacht, watching stunning sunsets, grilling jumbo prawns on his barbecue and sipping daiquiris, while he accesses his offshore account on his lap top or via his satellite phone.

What part of the world appeals to you the most? Perhaps it's not the Caribbean that interests you. Then why not travel to the south of France and visit your money? Imagine the trip. You're flying in first class on Air France, your destination? Provence, the South of France.

While the plane is still sitting on the ground and all the coach passengers are bumping into each other, trying to stuff their bags in the overhead bins and scrambling to sit in a seat that is far too small, the flight attendant is asking you what *you* would like to drink; a fine Cabernet perhaps?

While you wait for your wine, you stretch out in a soft leather recliner that's almost large enough for two. Soon after the flight takes off a three-course meal is served with crisp white linen napkins and wine glasses made of Baccarat crystal. As you savor the filet mignon and fois gras, a movie screen five feet across drops down in front of you in preparation for the evening's entertainment. Before the movie begins, you open your laptop to check on your offshore account. All of your statements are available with current balances along with any other information you wish. When you are finished reviewing your account, you turn off your laptop and all of the information disappears into cyberspace. You have no paper records to keep track of or for others to look at. All of the information about your account resides secretly and safely in the bank's computer. When you arrive at your hotel in Provence, you notice that there are chocolates and a hand-written thank you card personalized to you, resting on your pillow and your bed has already been turned down.

In the morning you decide to visit your private banker and talk with one of the officers to review your account. Later that afternoon you may choose to lie on the warm white sand beach  and do nothing. Then you decide that the following day, you will go to your yacht, take along some friends and go for a cruise where you will treat them to a fine French Champagne and delicate appetizers throughout the day. The point to all of this is that there are thousands upon thousands of people who live like this. They enjoy all the best that life has to offer.

Their assets and wealth are in an impenetrable fortress free from prying eyes or from those who would take it in any way, shape or form, whether that be a creditor, collection agency or an ex-spouse.

Exchange rates

Because unfavorable fluctuations in foreign currency can erode your portfolio, we always suggest that you keep your assets in the currency in which you ultimately plan to spend it.

Imagine making 25% on your Yen-based investments only to have the Yen drop 35% in value against the dollar? Unless you are a sophisticated investor who thoroughly understands foreign currencies, keep your assets in U.S. dollars. If you want to buy a foreign fund that doesn't offer a U.S. dollar fund, then you could hedge back to the U.S. dollar. You would buy a fund in Hong Kong dollars, for example, but you would hedge it back through a derivative to U.S. dollars; a sort of insurance policy  that you buy that protects you against a drop in any given foreign currency. You pay a small premium for that, but it's a tiny amount in comparison to the safety of knowing that you're not going to experience any currency losses. And once again, if your portfolio is heavily invested in stocks, a prudent investor might want to diversify those assets across other equities including cash, bonds, real estate or whatever you are comfortable with. I always suggest that people diversify not only across industries but globally as well. In other words, don't put all your eggs in one basket.

In terms of investing globally, offshore banking officials offer far more expertise than your local U.S. bank. Offshore banks understand these markets because they handle assets from all over the world.

Tools

Offshore companies

Just as you have done with your estate planning and your asset protection here in the United States, you can use your offshore accounts to build the same type of fortress, only more so.

Yes, you can open a bank account and just put cash into it. Yes you can build a portfolio of various investments such as stocks, bonds, mutual funds, etc. However, just as you might have taken your personal and business assets and put them into a domestic corporation, you can form an offshore Limited Company or other corporate form. This is how you would begin to build further layers of protection. First you would start with an offshore bank account. This account would hold cash and securities. Then you would form a corporate entity, which would own those assets of the bank account. Now you have two layers of protection and privacy. Not only is the bank account completely secret, your corporation has stock certificates in bearer form. There is no public record of your ownership of this corporation.

For added privacy the offshore company has nominee officers and directors. That means that the public record in the offshore jurisdiction only shows the name of our agent, usually an attorney there. Therefore if anyone were to attempt to inquire about ownership through legal means, they could only find the names of the nominees, and these nominees only know the people in our law office; they don't even have any record or knowledge of the true owners of the company.

The offshore nominees and their agents also provide services you may need. For example mail forwarding, invoicing, telephone messages, fax, e-mail and of course, all of this is under strict privacy.

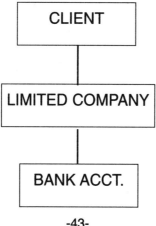

Now we need to to give your company a name. How about "East-West Trading Ltd. or Global Equities Inc. By using a company name, all transfers in and out of your company remain private. You can actually use your company for international business; perhaps set up a web site, use e-mail or do business throughout the world using your offshore company. The possibilities are endless. You can even use your offshore company to hold your brokerage account and trade all of your stocks, mutual funds and investments through your offshore bank's secure Internet web-site.

Tools
International trusts

Our third offshore building block would be to form a trust. The offshore trust is an umbrella over the corporation and the bank account. The trust's sole assets are the shares that it owns in the company and the company's sole asset is the bank account. Now, you also have two-way privacy and two-way secrecy. When the trust company looks down, it only sees the company and when the bankers look up, they also only see the company! Both the bank account and the trust are invisible to each other.

The next step would be to appoint a trustee to oversee and manage the trust in the event that you become disabled, die or are under any type of compulsion to turn over assets.

In addition to a trustee, you would appoint a trust protector committee to oversee the trustee. This committee could be your family members or whomever you choose.

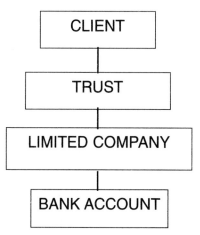

It might even be best to appoint a three or five member committee to insure a majority vote on any issues you deem important. If you were to become disabled, this committee and trustee would continue to pay your bills and manage your assets. Suppose you were sued and a court of law compelled you to reveal your assets? In this case you could reveal that your assets were owned by an offshore trust that you had no control over.

Let's further suppose, a court issued an order for you to turn over those assets. You would then invoke the "duress clause," in your trust; one that you put into your instructions to the trustees when you set up the trust. At this time the committee and a trustee would control the assets, you would have no control over them and therefore you or they could not turn them over to anyone or any court.

In addition, as long as you are under duress such as a judgment creditor seeking to attach your assets, you can still enjoy the lifestyle you have become accustomed to. The trustee would still pay your bills including your living expenses and you could still withdraw money through ATMs. The trust's assets could still be available to you if those are the wishes you dictated to the trustee and the committee. You did not dictate that they turn over assets to any other person or entity with the exception of yourself and your family And remember, the instructions and the trust are private documents, not available to any public source, including creditors.

In addition to the "duress clause," there is another vehicle available to you to add yet another layer of protection and that is the "flight clause," which you would also add into your instructions.

With this clause you are free to change the jurisdiction of your offshore bank account, company or trust at any time. There are more than thirty safe and legitimate offshore jurisdictions and these transfers are quite common and simple. If, in the very unlikely event, a judgment creditor were able to discover your offshore structure, you would just transfer the trust and the company and its assets to any one of the other locations. But since it is very difficult to locate your offshore account, only the most aggressive judgment creditor would take the time and expend the financial resources necessary.

By using the "flight clause," if a creditor had obtained a very large judgment against you and did, indeed try to locate your assets, by moving jurisdictions, you effectively extend the time frame, from the date of the judgment, so far out in time, that most creditors just give up trying to attach your assets.

Also creditor attorneys often work on a contingency basis. This means the attorney does not receive a penny for his or her work, unless a settlement is reached and assets are retrieved or turned over to the attorney. How many attorneys are going to spend years of their own time and thousands upon thousands of dollars of their own money trying to locate protected offshore assets? Remember, the older a debt is, the more difficult it becomes to collect.

There is a saying, "Wait long enough and things will change." Remember Imelda Marcos of the Philippines? Her assets were fully protected and although she had millions of dollars in judgments against her and had to leave the country, her assets were always intact. Years later, things changed in the Philippines and she became a congresswoman and was able to enjoy the wealth she had protected years before.

In the scenario we have been describing, at some point in the future if you wanted to settle with any given creditor for whatever reason, you would then be in a better position to control the negotiations for a settlement. At that future point in time, having spent years looking for your assets, it is likely a creditor would accept a settlement of five or ten cents on the dollar because they would have nothing to lose at that point.

There is another facet of law that can be a powerful tool to protect your assets; it's called the "statute of limitations." These statutes vary from country to country. They put time limits on how long a creditor can wait to initiate a lawsuit. In the United States it can be as long as seven years. That means that the creditor would have to initiate any legal action to overturn conveyances within that statutory period. In the jurisdictions we use, the statute of limitations are as short as one year. So let's do a "what if "scenario. Let's suppose someone sues you and wins a judgment. Generally speaking a lawsuit requires a great deal of time involved in initiating the service of process, filing answers, interrogatories, depositions, settlement conferences and the like, and this is all before the actual trial even *begins.* Then we have the trial, motions, appeals, etc., even more delays.

Typically, these things can take a year and much more. During these phases, including the trial, the creditor is not allowed to discover assets, because the trial has not yet concluded. The plaintiff does not have a judgment so there is no legal authority to question you about your assets. A creditor attorney can only begin to look for assets, once they have won a trial and obtained a judgment against you.

The next phase will be that period of years that it takes to find your assets. In most cases all of these laborious and expensive aspects take many, many years. However, even if a judgment creditor was to locate your assets, he would have to pursue the case in the offshore jurisdiction. That would mean he would have to sue you again in that jurisdiction. This means flying witnesses to far away places, the cost of an attorney's time and expenses, and other costly maneuvers which are unlikely to happen. Even if it did, by the time your creditor hired an attorney in that foreign jurisdiction (which he must legally do), the one-year statute of limitations would have long passed and their lawsuit would be rejected by that jurisdiction's court.

Now, let's take our "what if" scenario one-step further. Suppose for whatever *highly unlikely* reason, a creditor was able to accomplish all of this within one year and had the resources and time to pursue the case in a foreign jurisdiction (a scenario that would have to include only the largest settlements; cases involving millions of dollars), now the legal concept of "burden of proof" would enter into the equation. There are three types of "burdens of proof." At the lowest level, there is what is called, "a preponderance of evidence," which means that in order to find you liable, a jury must find that a preponderance of evidence points to your liability. This generally means that the plaintiff would have to prove that his case is 51% more likely than your case to be the correct decision.

The second level of proof necessary to find a defendant liable would be what is referred to as, "clear and convincing evidence." In this situation, the burden rises to 75%. This standard is mostly for cases involving fraud.

The highest level of evidence needed to convict or win a judgment is referred to as, "beyond a reasonable doubt." You will remember the O.J. Simpson case wherein he was acquitted in a criminal case because the plaintiff failed to prove that he was guilty beyond a reasonable doubt. However, Simpson subsequently lost his "civil" case because the plaintiff was able to establish a lower level of proof, "a preponderance of evidence" pointing to his liability.

In this last scenario (beyond a reasonable doubt) the burden rises to about 99%. The point to all of this is that in the offshore jurisdictions we use, the plaintiff must prove their case "beyond a reasonable doubt," making it even more difficult to obtain a judgment. It is appropriate here to reiterate what I have already said several times. We represent clients whose assets have been obtained *legally*. It is our goal to help clients protect those assets against any and all onslaughts.

Taxes

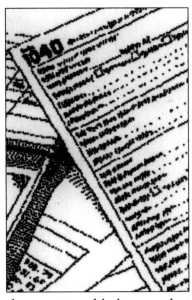

Another misnomer about offshore banking is the thought that your income is non-taxable. Meaning the interest you earn on cash deposits or the capital gains you achieve through stock sales or whatever other investments you have made, would not be taxable. It is true that the country where the offshore account resides does not tax this income, but you are generally liable for U.S. taxes. Just as someone from the UK is not liable for U.S. taxes on certain income in his or her bank here, that person *is* liable for UK taxes back home.

However, offshore banks do not issue 1099 forms to the IRS, so you are on the honor system to report these gains or earnings. You will get a statement at the end of the year for your own personal files and you would use these to report this income. However, keep one more thing in mind; your tax papers are strictly between you and the Internal Revenue Service. Your tax filing is a private matter and no one else can see a copy of these filings, unless you give it to them.

One way to minimize the taxes on your offshore account would be to defer liquidation of stocks thereby taking advantage of the lesser capital gains taxation rate. You can further defer gains by setting up an offshore annuity that defers the tax on investments until liquidation or until bringing it back into the U.S. Just remember, you should always file the necessary forms with the IRS so you can safely bring your investments or money home when and if you choose.

Many of the companies that are set up in offshore jurisdictions follow the previous rules with regard to taxation. However, there are some international companies, which have reduced tax burdens or do not have any tax liabilities at all in the U.S. These companies are usually export oriented or have mostly beneficial owners overseas. Also, if more than ten U.S. shareholders join together to operate an offshore company, taxes are usually not due until profits are repatriated.

A good example of offshore tax savings involves one of our clients who is a writer and a publishing consultant. He travels extensively and his business is conducted, for the most part, over the Internet. His corporation is in the Caribbean however, it does business with people all over the globe who pay the company with their credit cards or through wire transfers to the offshore bank. Further, family members who live overseas own the corporation. All payments up to $75,000 per year to the writer are made tax-free as long as he is a resident of a foreign country or spends at least 330 days a year overseas. A married couple in the same context would be able to exclude up to $150,000 per year on foreign-earned income. Since all of his work is e-mailed to his clients and the corporation is in the Caribbean, our client can really work anywhere in the world and save a bundle on taxes.

Today, many businesses that are consulting or service-based can be operated completely over the Internet quite easily. In fact, some very famous and extremely wealthy people have even given up their U.S. citizenship's to move offshore along with their accounts in order to avoid paying U.S. taxes; a practice known as expatriation.

In the words of Judge Learned Hand, "Over and over again, courts have ruled that there is nothing sinister in so arranging one's affairs as to keep taxes as low as possible. Everybody does so; rich or poor, and all do right, for nobody owes any public duty to pay more than the law demands—taxes are enforced exactions, not voluntary contributions. To demand more in the name of morals is mere cant."

You could fill a Boeing 747 with the wealthy U.S. citizens who have taken on foreign citizenship rather than submit to what Judge Learned Hand called "enforced exactions" at a level that amounts to virtual confiscation.

Some of the expatriates of recent years include Michael Dingman, Chairman of Abex and a Ford Motor Company Director who is now a citizen of the Bahamas. Billionaire John (Ippy) Dorrance III, an heir to the Campbell Soup fortune now lives in Ireland. He also resides in the Bahamas and in Wyoming.

J. Mark Mobius, a very successful emerging market investment manager is a citizen of Germany and resides in Hong Kong. Kenneth Dart, an heir to Dart Container and his family's $1 billion fortune is a citizen of Belize and Ted Arison, founder of Carnival Cruise Lines was an Israeli citizen. All of these people and many, many others share one common happiness; none of them pay any U.S. taxes, income or otherwise and they all live in beautiful, interesting countries. The United States is not necessarily the best place in the world to live for everyone. For some, it's just a great place to visit, but they wouldn't want to live here and pay the taxes!

Your estate taxes would be handled the same way in an offshore trust, as they would in a domestic trust with the added benefits of even more privacy and secrecy. Any conveyance to an offshore trust, considered a grantor trust, is not subject to gift tax and does not use any of your lifetime credits. Transfers of real estate, boats, cars and any other personal property generally will not result in any taxable event, so you incur no additional tax on transfers locally. Also, all of your estate planning methods, A-B trusts, etc. are still effective. As you can see offshore planning offers many benefits without any changes to your tax situation.

An impenetrable fortress!

Review

Estate planning, Domestic asset protection
and Offshore asset protection

1. We have achieved our goals of: secrecy, privacy, safety and convenience and helped to structure your taxes correctly
2. We have used the tools of private banking, offshore companies and international trusts
3. We have taken your family, asset and wealth protection to the highest level—an impenetrable fortress
4. We have set up your private bank account which you, and only you, can access via the Internet. You now have an offshore credit card, ATM access, checking, wire transfer capability and all the other routine banking services you would find here in the U.S. In addition, you can now use your private banker to invest in any securities you wish
5. You now have a wonderful place to visit your assets.
6. You've learned about favorable exchange rates
7. We have also set up an offshore company and an international trust.

8. All of these tools have made it nearly impossible
   for creditors or any one else to find your assets
   and even in the highly unlikely event they did,
   you have learned about duress clauses, flight
   clauses, statute of limitations and burdens of
   proof
9. We have discussed the tax situation and the transfer
   of assets

ASSET PROTECTION
GLOBAL STRUCTURE

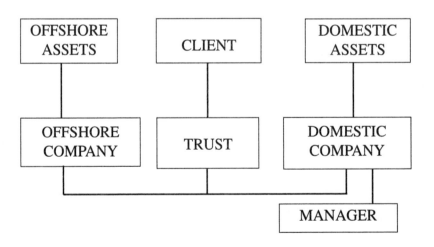

Chapter Four
Timing and Planning
Getting started

We have now discussed Estate planning, Living Trusts, Asset Protection, Limited Partnerships, LLCs and Corporations, all of which protect your assets and provide privacy. We have also discussed tax reduction strategies. Remember, high taxes, lawsuits, seizures and liens are the penalties you will experience *only* as a result of your poor planning and/or timing. Certainly, no one expects to die tomorrow, but people do die unexpectedly all the time. People also become ill at the worst possible times. No one expects to go through a divorce either, but more than half of the people who are married this year, will eventually be divorced. And of course, no one wants to be involved in a lawsuit, have an employee be involved in an accident and or wants to be the victim of an accident.

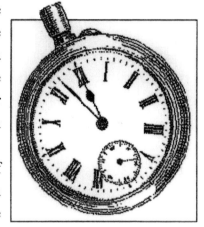

The point is, that all of these things can and do happen unexpectedly. So I would like to discuss the *timing* of your plans. These kinds of plans are for the honest, prudent, intelligent, person who has worked hard to earn a good living and has acquired a certain amount of wealth. This same prudent person would be well served to "plan ahead." In other words, do it before you need to!

With regard to lawsuits and your asset protection, there is the legal concept of "fraudulent conveyance," which is important to mention.

This means that if you convey (change title to) any asset during your lifetime for the purposes of avoiding a creditor (creditor as the result of a lawsuit, bad debt, whatever), this action on your part *could* be considered fraudulent, which could result in the loss of those assets and even additional legal sanctions. The courts have interpreted some transfers from which "you diminish your ability to satisfy that creditor," to be possible fraud. This law is based on *intent* and that is a very important word within this concept.

If you are notified of a lawsuit and you immediately begin to transfer all your assets to your brother, you may find yourself in further legal trouble. You need to start building your walls and your fortress now—when you *don't* need them. Remember that everything you are going to transfer is for the purposes of estate planning, and it will all go into trusts and companies. Our purpose for conveying these assets is to protect your children, for legal tax advantages and for the purposes of setting up a smart business plan. The by-product of all this is that all of your assets and privacy are protected. What you are telling the world is that you are doing prudent planning.

Now, suppose two or three years have passed since you did your prudent planning. All of your structures are in place but unfortunately, you are involved in an accident, or someone sues you. Your timely planning two, three or more years ago, is going to provide you with a powerful position with which to defend yourself and your assets. In other words, could you have known three years ago, that you would be sued today? No one could argue intent. Why would you have set up something so long ago anticipating a lawsuit? "Remote in time. Remote in intent," is the key concept.

Planning ahead and setting up your asset protection in the manner we have been discussing discourages costly and lengthy lawsuits. Even if there is no basis for a lawsuit against you, a long court battle can be expensive nevertheless.

Let me demonstrate my point by using this example: Suppose you are worth $5 million and you have done all that we have discussed to this point. Further suppose that you are now sued by someone. Let's use the instance of an automobile accident. You have slammed into someone who has sustained a lot of soft tissue injuries and they sue you using a Personal Injury Attorney who is going to take the case on a contingency basis. In other words, the attorney will pay all of the out of pocket expenses and not charge his client anything unless he wins the lawsuit, in which case; he may receive anywhere from 30% to 40% of what he or she was able to recover from you.

The person you ran into has now given your name and the name of your insurance company to this attorney and the attorney has agreed to take the case on a contingency basis. The first thing this attorney is going to do, is to investigate you and find out how much you are worth or what your assets are, because he or she wants to sue you for much more than your insurance policy covers.

After reviewing all of the public records and other various sources that attorneys use, your name does not turn up on anything. You don't personally own a home, a car or even much of a bank account.

However, you have done something quite brilliant. Let's suppose you do have a savings account with $50,000 in it (keeping in mind that you are worth a few million dollars, this is not a very significant amount). I call this a "self cannibalizing" account. This is what is going to happen. The attorney is going to find that account. *He* is going to see that this is your *only* asset. He will now become a salesman for *your cause. He will plead your case to his client for you.* How? You are going to tell the attorney who is trying to sue you, that this is all the money you have. If the person who is suing you will accept this amount as full settlement, he or see can have it. If he or she wants to fight it out in court, you will use this money to pay *your* attorney to fight them—the longer the battle rages, the more the $50,000 diminishes, until finally there is nothing left.

The attorney is going to tell his client to take the $50,000 because that is all there is and because he will want the 30% or 40% of it as payment for his or her services.

Sometimes that initial lawsuit serves as a wake up call to a client calling on him to strengthen his plan further before a much more serious lawsuit hits him.

Our firm has set up over 5,000 asset protection plans and our client's success rates is close to 100%, meaning either a complete win with nothing being paid out, or at least a settlement for a greatly reduced amount.

Chapter Five
Other strategies
Keeping it all

Marital agreements

Pre-nuptial agreements are quite common today however, a growing number of people are finding that a post-nuptial agreement can work just as well.

This could be an alternative for you depending upon several factors. As an example a post-nuptial agreement might have allowed Gary and Lorna Wendt to have avoided a lot of unpleasant battles. Wendt was CEO of GE Capital. When he offered his wife a divorce settlement of $10 million. She countered that his assets were worth $100 million and that she was entitled to half of that. The dispute was bitterly fought out in a Connecticut court, and might not even have occurred had the couple initiated a postnuptial agreement.

A postnup, like a prenup is intended to protect the financial interests of both spouses in the event of a divorce or death; most often when one partner has substantially more assets than the other. The question is, why *after* instead of *before*? Usually it's because the couple's financial circumstances change after they have been married and most often because both partners feel it is prudent to plan ahead while they are still talking to each other (remember planning and timing?).

A post nuptial can serve a variety of purposes. The usual idea is to let spouses keep personal assets separate so that their children from another marriage can inherit them and of course it can spell out what each spouse gets if they split up. That can be particularly valuable in any of the community property states. In these states, any property acquired *during* your marriage will be split evenly without a pre or post-nuptial. A post-nuptial can help ease anxieties on both sides and will allow both parties to override the applicable divorce laws in these states by deciding exactly how *you,* not the state, wants your assets divided.

A pre-nuptial does not have to be entirely about money and assets either. Several years ago a matrimonial lawyer in New Jersey was involved in a pre-nuptial negotiation that stipulated how many times a week the couple would have sex. You can include most any wishes that are a concern to either party in a pre or post-nuptial agreement.

The asset protection attributes of the postnuptial agreement is that we can place all of the valuable cash and equity-rich assets with the least lawsuit-prone spouse. The husband may be a physician, real estate developer or perhaps a businessman concerned about potential lawsuits. He would much rather have these assets go to his wife and children than a judgment creditor. So we can set up an agreement wherein the house, cars, rental property and liquid assets go to the wife and the business (goodwill), professional licenses old car and clothes go to the husband (a split not unlike many divorces you have heard of!). Actually we value the business goodwill and professional licenses highly enough to really make the financial arrangement a relatively reasonable division. The husband's wealth would now lie in intangibles; not particularly desirable to a judgment creditor.

Of course, most husbands ask me the question, "What if my wife divorces me, do I lose all my assets?" The answer to that is that we can include a clause in the agreement that states that in case of a divorce, at least one-half of the estate reverts back to the husband. So you can see, we really have covered all the necessary concerns.

Tax collections

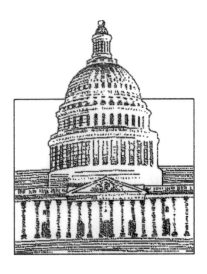

Most of this book has been devoted to planning ahead, planning for your estate and planning for the protection of your assets and wealth.

Unfortunately some people procrastinate and do not plan for potential financial problems. A lack of planning can often result in being penalized either through a lawsuit, a tax burden or even just an overwhelming debt burden. However, even if these traumatic experiences do occur, there are remedies that can keep you from losing everything.

The first situation would involve a person or a couple that have amassed a tax liability that is far beyond any reasonable effort to pay. Years ago, the Internal Revenue Service implemented a program called "Offers in Compromise." The idea was for the IRS to settle up and allow taxpayers that had been hounded for years by collection agents, to start over with a clean slate.

Recently, at the direction of Congress, the IRS loosened its criteria for accepting Offers in Compromise, which are formal pleas from cash-strapped taxpayers to pay less than they owe—typically 10 to 20 cents on the dollar. The taxpayers could regain their financial stability and the IRS would stop trying to collect uncollectible taxes.

Now, even state tax agencies have begun to implement similar proceedings. The states no longer reject 95% of settlement offers as they once did. The states have also become more generous with installment plans.

What would constitute the need for an Offer in Compromise?" Essentially, if your taxes are well beyond your ability to *ever* pay, even through an installment plan, you should consider this alternative. An attorney/CPA can help you with the paperwork. However, keep in mind, that if you own a home and the title is in your name and there is any equity in that home, the IRS can force the sale of that asset or any other assets, to try to satisfy your tax debt prior to accepting any Offer in Compromise.

That is why we recommend setting up a plan for transferring ownership of assets, hopefully way before you get into this type of situation. Asset protection, properly implemented, works even when dealing with the IRS. Remember, the IRS is the largest and *most efficient* collection agency in the world!

Bankruptcy

It should not be a stigma, nor should you feel guilty, if at some point in your life, you find that you must avail yourself of the U.S. bankruptcy laws. They are intended to protect individuals from creditors. Many very bright and successful people have utilized this option. Very often, finding yourself in need of bankruptcy protection, is the result of conditions outside your control. All of the forms of Bankruptcy are intended to give people a fresh start.

There are three bankruptcy options, they are: Chapter 13, wherein you develop a plan to partially satisfy your creditors with a payment plan over many years. Chapter 11, a form of bankruptcy primarily for businesses to reorganize. Chapter 7, the type of bankruptcy wherein you can discharge most or even all of your debts entirely.

Filing for bankruptcy puts an immediate and automatic stop on your creditor's collection attempts. In a Chapter 7 filing many of your debts will be canceled without any further repayment. In some cases, this can include some taxes you might owe.

In some cases you may have to surrender some of your "non exempt" property. Property that is exempt and need not be surrendered would be some motor vehicles, clothing, household furnishings, pensions and life insurance policies.

However, be careful, even bankruptcy requires prudent planning. I have seen too many people rush out and file bankruptcy too soon without proper guidance, only to *still* lose their homes, property, everything and still on top of that they often still owe taxes and have undischarged debts.

With advanced planning, asset protection can provide a structure where even after bankruptcy, some assets are still intact for the benefit of your family and loved ones. And, with very good planning, we can make sure you walk away not owing the IRS or the state anything! Again, remember that *timing is critical*, all planning must be done as early as possible.

Retirement plans

Today, it seems nearly everyone has an IRA, 401K or some other sort of pension plan, and many ask the question, "Am I protected?" The answer is yes *and* no. 401Ks and pension plans set up under Federal law (ERISA) are usually protected. However, IRAs are usually only protected under state laws and those laws vary widely; anywhere from absolutely no protection, to protected for reasonable retirement needs. So, part of our strategy is to move the unprotected portion to a fully protected strategy using companies, pension plans and custodial accounts. Be careful, plan early. These are your retirement funds that are at stake.

Collateralization and encumbrances

If you own property free and clear, you can imagine how attractive that would be to a judgment creditor. Now imagine that same property encumbered with a 1st, 2nd, 3rd mortgage and perhaps even a line of credit against it.

A $400,000 property encumbered by a traditional note to an institutional lender for 75% of the value, would be $300,000, which leaves $100,000 vulnerable. Now, what if we put a 2nd note for $150,000 payable to a domestic company, perhaps owned by an offshore company, on top of the 1st? A creditor would see a property over-encumbered by $50,000 negative equity, not an attractive target to try to attach.

Actually, the same thing can be done for personal property such as cars, boats, airplanes, motor homes, equipment, inventory and intangible property, i.e., trademarks, copyrights and patents, by using UCC filings under State Uniform Commercial codes. By filing a financing statement with the Secretary of State's office, similar encumbrances can make non-real estate assets an equally unattractive target. Of course these loans would have to be fully documented and enforceable, but only to our pre-selected companies.

Affordability

Planning that used to involve fees affordable only to the super rich, now are available and affordable to most everyone. Offshore planning has become more flexible and due to the large volume of business that we bring to international banks and trust companies, we are able to negotiate very favorable rates for clients. Costs will vary among clients with different needs. From the most basic of entities to a very complicated structure, all the fees and professional charges are usually paid for in the first few months of tax savings. Also, most clients, after being introduced to our professional planning, increase their yield on their portfolios by several points.

Whatever your needs, these methods are very flexible. Like all of the building blocks in this book, you can start with a very simple structure and build on to it to suit your needs. As your business grows, we can have your structure grow with you.

A caveat

Be aware that asset protection planning, particularly offshore planning is complex and should not be attempted as a "do-it-yourself" project. Too many people end up getting lost in multi-state and multi-jurisdictional laws, only to find out later that a licensed professional could have set up plans efficiently and properly. Today, many inexperienced sales people have set up companies via mail order or the Internet trying to promote "package deals" offering asset protection. These inexperienced people are, usually unlicensed and tend to operate out of a postal boxes. Do not share your valuable financial information with them. Too many people have been very disappointed with bogus arrangements and our office ends up spending *more time* unwinding asset protection plans that have been set up improperly.

Also, be careful with inexperienced attorneys who, as a sideline, only set up a few plans a year. They usually do not have the requisite tax background and do not subscribe to the necessary journals and research reports to be fully informed of the many changes in laws around the globe. This type of legal work requires that all forms, contracts and agreements are in perfect order.

You deserve the best help when dealing with your hard-earned wealth, particularly when family members are relying on you. Also, be very careful with promotions offering high returns, with very little risk. As you have heard many times, "If it sounds too good to be true....it probably isn't!"

Also, a very important rule to follow is to only discuss your planning with a *licensed attorney*. An accountant, tax preparer, paralegal, corporate agent, service center or management company, can be summoned to testify and turn over your confidential records. They have no privacy laws protecting you, unlike the Attorney-client privilege.

Only licensed attorneys enjoy the Attorney-client privilege protecting your privacy and your money. This privilege is *very* powerful.

Your asset protection plan is like a chain, it's only as strong as each individual link. Do not have any broken or weak links. All of your planning, discussions, memorandums and even your tax data should be protected by the Attorney-client privilege.

Conclusion

Setting up an asset protection plan is a very important process. Our office can help you get started by advising you on the best methods to reach your objectives. It is always better to do some pre-planning and not just start forming companies and then later try to figure out what to do with them. Feel free to contact our office for a private meeting or confidential phone conference. Our professional fee structure is reasonable and affordable.

Appendix
JURISDICTIONS

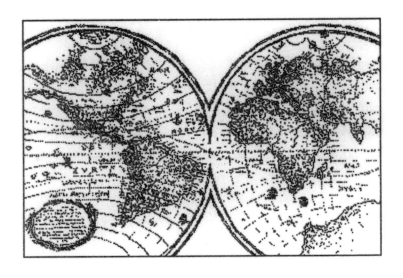

NEVADA

California Business Magazine, ranked Nevada's business climate #1 over-all and Money Magazine, ranked Nevada's tax climate the third lowest in state & local tax burden. Aside from the many amenities the state offers, Las Vegas provides a unique getaway environment found in few major metropolitan cities. Entertainment, gaming, a great climate and plenty of outdoor activities abound including: golf, boating, fishing, hunting and much more.

In addition, Las Vegas' airport is now a major International destination with frequent flights from just about every major metropolitan city in the world.

Nevada has no annual franchise tax and continues to be aggressive in seeking to encourage incorporations by providing a flexible, pro-management corporation law at a reasonable cost.

Currently, Nevada corporations offer outstanding and unique opportunities for privacy, protection, and profits by taking advantage of Nevada state tax and business laws in the following areas:

(1) No state corporate tax on profits or major annual fees, (2) No state personal income tax, (3) Protection from personal liability, (4) Stockholders' names are not public, (5) Directors can change corporate bylaws, (6) Stockholders are not required to be U.S. Citizens.

Nevada is an excellent location for companies and businesses.

DELAWARE

For over a Century, Delaware has been the location of choice for more than fifty percent of U.S. corporations. The reason for the continuation of this trend relates to the Delaware Corporation Law which is one of the most advanced and flexible statutes in the nation.

Currently, Delaware corporations offer outstanding and unique opportunities for privacy, protection, and profits by taking advantage of Delaware state tax and business laws in the following areas:

(1) No state corporate tax on interest or other investment income, (2) No state sales tax, (3) No taxes on business transactions, (4) No ad-valorem or value-added tax, (5) Directors can change corporate bylaws, (6) Stockholders are not required to be U.S. Citizens, and (7) A single person can be sole President, Secretary and Treasurer, (8) No Delaware capital shares or stock transfer taxes, (9) Liability of a shareholder of a Delaware corporation is limited to the value of the stock held in the corporation plus the corporate tax liability.

In addition a Delaware corporation may be based, headquartered and/or operated in any state or territory of the United States, or in any city in any country in the world, and you are not required to maintain a Delaware business office address aside from the address of your Delaware Registered Agent which is required for service of process.

Delaware has always been a favorite jurisdiction for corporations and business structures.

WYOMING

As one of the few states without a corporate income tax, Wyoming now joins Nevada as one of the premier incorporation centers in the United States to provide ease of use, liability protection, financial privacy and tax savings. Wyoming is a wonderful state to visit with a wealth of outdoor activities. Skiing, hunting and fishing are year round activities available to those individuals seeking clean air and a pristine physical environment.

In 1989, the Wyoming Legislature passed a new legislation that revolutionized their corporation laws. The advantages are in the following key areas:

(1) No corporate income tax and no tax on corporate shares, (2) No state franchise tax, (3) Annual fees are based on value of corporate assets within Wyoming, (4) One person may be all required corporate officers and directors, (5) Stockholders are not filed with the State, (6) No annual report is required until the anniversary of the incorporation date, (7) Articles of Incorporation may provide for unlimited stock without a requirement for stating par value, (8) Corporations with less than 50 shareholders are not required to have a board of directors meeting, minutes, and other paperwork associated with having a board, without affecting the corporate veil, (9) Wyoming statute has provisions for "bearer scrip" which can be used when stockholders capitalize the corporation in increments less than the par value of the stock.

All these attributes make Wyoming and excellent choice for company formation.

ANDORRA

Andorra is a small European country, located between Spain and France. The official language is Catalan, but French and Castilian Spanish are also commonly spoken. The climate is mild and temperate year round. The astounding coastal area of Spain known as the Costa Brava where Barcelona is located is just a half hour flight to the south from Andorra and Paris is little more than an hour away to the north.

This country has seven different banks that pride themselves on an extremely high level of secrecy. Also, there is a high level of due diligence with regard to all depositor's financial transactions. When making transfers of funds there are no exchange restrictions and no remittance. The Spanish peseta is the most widely circulated currency, followed by the French franc.

In Andorra three different types of mercantile societies can be formed. Two of the three types have limited liability, and the third one is a general partnership in which all partners are jointly and severally liable for the company's debts to the full of their personal assets.

Andorra does not have any tax treaties with other countries. Its laws avoid taxation on income from investments and capital. In Andorra, Trust matters are treated according to its traditional Old Catalan and Roman legal concepts of fiduciary status and trust.

This could be very convenient for offshore trusts, especially for the ones that are formed by individuals, where no minimum capital is required.

ANGUILLA

Anguilla is an island located in the eastern Caribbean approximately 500 miles east of Puerto Rico near Antigua and Barbuda. Like many of the idealic islands of the Caribbean, Anguilla has a year round warm climate with beautiful white sand beaches. There is an abundance of year round outdoor activities including: skiing, para-sailing, swimming, wind surfing, golf and much more. The water temperature averages 80 degrees year round.

Since the seventeenth century Anguilla has been a British dependent territory, considered a Crown colony. Therefore, Britain is responsible for its defense and foreign affairs. It is a stable country presided over by a British Governor, and its legal system is based on English Common Law with some local changes.

The official language is English and the official currency is the Eastern Caribbean Dollar. However, the US dollar circulates frequently for local commerce purposes. Furthermore, there are no exchange controls, money can be taken in or out of the island without any permission, and profits can be repatriated easily in any currency.

As with most of the rest Caribbean countries, Anguilla's economy is mainly based on tourism, offshore business, financial services and new construction. A remarkable characteristic of this country is that the taxes are based on consumption, not on income or productivity.

Anguilla can be a very advantageous, location since your automatically receives a fifty-year guarantee against future taxation. The only two requirements for this guarantee are that the settlor and beneficiaries must be non-residents of the island and the trust property might not include land.

This island is a very convenient place to invest and to do business.

ANTIGUA

Antigua is an island located in the Caribbean very near Anguilla, approximately 500 miles to the east of Puerto Rico. Again, this is a beautiful Caribbean country with warm year round temperatures. The capital and commercial center is St. Johns. The official language is English and the official currency is the Eastern Caribbean dollar. As with Anguilla, the legal system is based on British Common Law. It is an independent nation with political stability and a democratic government, based on the parliamentary system.

The economy is very stable and is principally based on tourism, business, banking services and the fact that it is a free trade zone. It is a member of the Caribbean Common Market (CARICOM).

This jurisdiction is recognized as a stable International Financial Center. The government encourages foreign investments. One of Antigua's specialties is its offshore banking system. There are quite a few international banks that have branches and subsidiaries on the Island.

As with other offshore jurisdictions, strict bank secrecy is regulated by the government. Repatriation of capital and profits are permitted and there are no exchange controls. Invoicing of offshore trade documents is allowed in any currency. Offshore businesses are exempt from corporate tax, trustee tax status, individual tax, withholding tax, capital gains, sales and other kinds of taxes.

To conclude, Antigua is excellent for investors seeking a safe and well-regulated place to do business.

AUSTRIA

Austria is located in the center of Europe to the east of Germany and to the northeast of Italy, which gives it a strategic geographic location for international trade matters. It extends from the Alps to the Danube River. Vienna, the capital is a wonderful, romantic city and is one of the permanent seats of the United Nations. Also, it is one of the wealthiest and most established members of the European Union.

Travel to Munich, Berlin, Switzerland and Milan Italy is quick and direct and if you are a skier, you will find some of the best skiing in Europe within the borders of this beautiful country.

Austria is a Republic with an elected President. The official language is German however, English is widely spoken as well. It follows the Roman law system, as most of the European countries do. It is politically and socially well established and this fact has contributed to making this country a stable and reliable jurisdiction for people who want to invest in Europe. Since Austria is an export-oriented country, it maintains a sophisticated foreign trade system.

Austria's economic system is based on a free market economy, with an emphasis on social factors favoring the economically less privileged sectors.

Finally, most of the foreign investors who are willing to establish a holding company in Austria, prefer the limited liability company because it requires lower capital, easier way to change the management, and less financial reporting obligations.

BAHAMAS

The Bahamas is a group of 70 islands, located in the Caribbean region, starting at approximately 50 miles east of Florida. The weather is temperate year round and there is an abundance of amenities including beautiful beaches, golf and gaming activities. Perhaps its strongest advantage is the fact that it is only minutes from Miami.

Nassau, the capital is also the commercial center. The official language is English and the official currency is the Bahamian Dollar, which is on par with the US dollar. Bahamian law is based on British Common Law with some local modifications. Even though it is an independent and democratic country, within the Commonwealth, a Governor-General is appointed by the British Government. However, the real head of the Government is the Prime Minister, who is elected by the population. Its economy is flexible and it has the ability to respond to international market changes quickly.

In the Bahamas there is no direct taxation either on income, capital gains, or estates for residents or non-residents. Furthermore, non-residents and offshore entities are not subject to any exchange control restrictions. Actually, they are free to operate international accounts inside or outside the Bahamas, and to enter into any transactions with non-residents. The banking system is well developed and has a long and rich tradition. Most of the Bahamian banks are subsidiaries of major world public banks and they deal almost exclusively (90%) in offshore operations. All banking transactions are protected by banking secrecy laws. This jurisdiction is a long established offshore area.

BARBADOS

Barbados is an island located in the southeastern part of the Caribbean approximately 500 miles northeast of Venezuela. As with most of the islands in this part of the world, such as nearby St. Lucia and Martinique, Barbados is a major tourist destination with gorgeous white sand beaches and year round warm temperatures.

English is the official language and the official currency is the Barbados dollar. Barbados is an independent country with a well-developed legal system based on the British Common Law. It is a member of several international organizations including the United Nations, the Organization of American States and the British Commonwealth.

The economy of this beautiful island is principally based on sugar production, tourism, agriculture and international financial services. Barbados has established a reputation as a world class international services center. It offers a variety of offshore facilities for international business companies and offshore banks.

Barbados has no capital gains tax, no accumulated profits tax, no estate and no gift tax. Furthermore, it has a stable legislation oriented to facilitate offshore entities, by providing guarantees against future taxation for periods between 15 and 30 years.

The banking system on this island is well-organized and established. It is easy to business there, the language is convenient, excellent communications, no tax policy, and it is a very beautiful place.

BELIZE

Belize is a small independent country, located on the eastern Caribbean coast of Central America. Its closest neighbors are Mexico to the north and Guatemala to the west. Although the official language is English, Spanish is also widely spoken.

The climate is warm year round and there is an abundance of recreational opportunities. Diving is a major tourist attraction. Cancun and Cozumel, two other beautiful tourist locations are within an hour's flight of Belize City. The official currency is the Belize dollar. It is a member of the United Nations and the British Commonwealth, and its legal system is based on the British Common Law supplemented by local legislation.

The Government maintains an environment that encourages investments by both local and foreign investors. For example, there are fiscal incentives for investments in the form of tax holidays and duty exemptions, and there is a commercial free zone. Furthermore, the government supports various categories of business ownership: Joint Ventures and Cooperatives, Partnerships, Sole Proprietorships, Private Companies, Public Investment Companies, International Business Companies, and Trust Funds.

An asset protection trust formed in Belize, is protected from foreign court judgments as well as from claims under Belize's bankruptcy legislation.

Belize is a good country for foreign investments. Clients can enjoy complete privacy and confidentiality regarding all their business dealings.

BERMUDA

Bermuda is a small island located east of Miami, less than an hour's flying time. The official language is English and the official currency is the Bermuda dollar. It is Britain's oldest existing colony. Britain is responsible for the island's foreign affairs, internal security and defense. It has a stable government (a self-governing British dependency), a sophisticated infrastructure, and a strong economy. The major industries are tourism and international business.

Bermuda is a well-known vacation destination and there is an abundance of available recreational activities including: beautiful balmy, white sand beaches, gaming, golf, para-sailing and even Polo.

This jurisdiction is well-recognized as a unique and sophisticated international business center. Currently this \country is essentially tax-free. There are no income tax, gift, estate, business, value added, corporate, non-resident, capital gains, sales, withholding, or accumulated profit taxes. Bermuda provides complete privacy since reporting of income or ownership is not required by any government agency. There are no exchange controls or other financial restraints imposed upon a company. Furthermore, through the use of trusts and private corporations, individuals can shelter their assets from several forms of taxation in their declared domicile.

The banking industry in Bermuda is well-known, well-developed, very efficient and highly regarded. It also has acquired a reputation for integrity and fiscal solidity. And it is a beautiful island on which to do business.

BRITISH VIRGIN ISLANDS

The British Virgin Islands is a group of 60 Caribbean islands. The closest country is Puerto Rico, only 60 miles to the east. The largest and most populated island is Tortola, which is also the business and commercial center. At present, this group of islands is a British colony. Britain appoints a Governor who is responsible for defense, internal security, external affairs, the civil service, the administration of the courts and finance. This group of islands is a very popular U.S. tourist destination and as with most of the Caribbean countries it has a wealth of recreational opportunities. Temperatures are warm year round and there are certainly no lack of beaches and sunshine.

The British Virgin Islands are quite stable both politically and economically. The official and only spoken language is English. The legal system is based on English Common Law, with local modifications. The official currency is the US dollar and there are no local exchange control regulations. The two main industries are tourism and offshore finance. This jurisdiction offers maximum security of assets, including the possibility to transfer domicile, abilities to transfer assets to another company, trust, association or partnership, and to merge with another British Virgin Island's company or with a foreign corporation in another country.

The British Virgin Islands has a very strong banking system. All banks have to follow the Banking License Guidelines proposed by Britain.

This is a perfect jurisdiction for people who are looking to invest in a location that offers confidentiality and anonymity, since it offers non-residents complete privacy.

CAYMAN ISLANDS

The Cayman Islands is a group of three islands located in the Caribbean, 500 miles south of Florida. This group of islands is a British colony, with a Governor selected by the Crown. Its legal system is based on English Common Law. The official language is English and the official currency is the Caymanian dollar. There is no exchange control. Its economy is very strong, is politically stable, has excellent infrastructure, and has modern legal, accountancy and banking services.

There are no taxes on income or profits, capital, wealth, property, sales, estates taxes, or inheritances. Offshore business is important to the Cayman Islands. At present large, long-established, and well-known companies are running businesses in this country.

Cayman Trusts operate under modern law. There are no restrictions in regard to who will settle funds in a trust. The deed covering the trust can be signed in any country, but it has to be filed with the Trust Registrar. Trusts are supervised by the Government, which ensure absolute confidentiality about the information given to the Registrar. The trust can be established with or without a settlor. Many of the main banks in the world have subsidiary and branch banking operations in this jurisdiction, which specializes in handling trust for their clients.

This jurisdiction is considered an excellent location for world operations. It has a well-developed communication's systems, there are no taxes whatsoever, the banking system is strong and secure, and the people are cooperative and friendly.

COOK ISLANDS

The Cook Islands is a group of 15 islands located in the South Pacific between Tahiti and Samoa. The official language is English and the official currency is the New Zealand dollar. The legal system is based on British Common Law with some local regulations.

It has a self-government in free association with New Zealand, which is responsible for the Island's international relations and defense. And it is a member of the British Commonwealth. The economy has grown considerably in the past 20 years, principally in the areas of tourism, financial services, and aquaculture.

This jurisdiction is recognized as an international financial center. The government gives high priority to the off-shore financial sector. International companies are exempt from any form of taxation including capital gains tax, capital issue tax, withholding tax, and stamp duties. Furthermore, there are no exchange controls on any currency or financial restrictions on the movement of money to or from the Island.

The trust concept is regulated by the Cook Island's legislation. In particular, an offshore trust can be created using a resident trustee company as agent or trustee. Furthermore, the company can be either a sole trustee or a co-trustee. Here the trustee is able to appoint an asset manager who is responsible for managing the trust assets commonly in a different country. The Cook Islands offer various incentives to international investors including very competitive costs and fees–and excellent location to do business.

COSTA RICA

The Republic of Costa Rica is located between Panama and Nicaragua. It is considered the most "westernized" nation in Central America. It separates the waters of the Pacific Ocean from the Caribbean Sea. The official language is Spanish, although English is widely spoken, especially in the business area. The official currency is the Colon, which is one of the most stable currencies in Latin America. It has a very strong democratic government, with the President as both the chief of state and the head of government, and it enjoys political stability. In addition, this government has been an outstanding example of democracy, which has been followed for more than forty years.

Since the early 19th Century, tourism has been the leading industry in the country, followed by the coffee and banana industries. Manufacturing is also an important industry.

Many attractive incentives are offered by the Costa Rica government to foreign investors. It has an excellent well-developed banking system. Foreigners can invest with the nationalized banking system, offshore banks, private banks, or finance companies. It has the largest stock exchange in Central America, which is regulated by the National Securities Commission (the counterpart of the U.S. Securities and Exchange Commission). It is not a requirement to be a resident to own or manage a business in the country. Furthermore, Costa Rica offers many tax advantages to investors. There are no capital gains taxes and high interest-bearing bank accounts are tax-free as well. This ia a convenient jurisdiction for international investors.

CYPRUS

The Island of Cyprus is located in the Mediterranean Sea, 500 miles from Greece. Because of its strategic location, it is a cross-roads between Europe, Middle East, Asia and Northern Africa. Even though the official languages are Greek and Turkish, English is widely spoken and is commonly used in commerce. The official currency is the Cypriot pound. Its legal system is based on British Common Law. Cyprus has been an independent nation since 1960, with a presidential system of government. It is a member of the United Nations, the British Commonwealth and the Council of Europe.

Cyprus is one of the main business centers in the Eastern Mediterranean region and it is rapidly turning into an offshore financial and commercial center. It has an open free market economy. The banking services are highly rated and there are very active branches of International Banks. Considerable reductions are offered to foreign investors on their income tax obligations, and also total exemption of the normal individual tax rates. There are no exchange control restrictions for offshore entities, and they can freely operate external or local accounts inside or outside the island and enter into any transactions with non-residents. Furthermore, non-residents are able to freely keep balances in any foreign currency. It has enjoyed a free trade zone since 1975.

In conclusion, this jurisdiction offers various advantages for international investors, especially for those seeking a country with such a strategic location.

GIBRALTAR

Gibraltar is a small country located on the southern tip of Spain and close to the north coast of Africa. The official language is English but most of the country is fluent in both English and Spanish. Since 1704, Gibraltar has been a British dependent territory. Therefore, Britain is responsible for the defense, foreign issues, financial stability and internal security. However, Gibraltar is responsible for its own internal government. Since it is a British dependent territory, it is a member of the European Union. The legal system is based on English common and statute law with some local modifications. The currency is the Gibraltar pound. There are no foreign exchange regulations.

This banking sector provides services to local and offshore clients, and these banks specialize in private banking services and investment services to companies or individuals who are non-residents. Banking confidentiality is enforced by law.

As a common law jurisdiction, Gibraltar law recognizes the concept of a Trust and gives it full legal effect. Gibraltar law does not apply any capital gains tax, sales, inheritance or wealth taxes. Other taxes such as income, corporation and withholding taxes are not applied to individuals and companies that are non-residents.

Some advantages to using this jurisdiction would be: stable government, good geographical location and communications, absence of any exchange control restrictions, exemptions from domestic taxes for certain categories of companies and attractive fiscal incentives for non-resident companies or individuals.

HONG KONG

Hong Kong is located on the southeastern coast of China. Even though the native languages are Cantonese and Mandarin, English is the official language. The official currency is the Hong Kong dollar. It enjoys political stability, based on a democratic government and a strong economy. It is considered the financial center of southern China and Asia. Its legal system is based on English Common Law.

Hong Kong is one of the world's leading centers for trade and commerce. The offshore specialties of Hong Kong are international holding companies, fund management and an international banking and finance center. This country is the ninth largest international banking center in the world with respect to the volume of external transactions. It also has one of the largest representations of international banks in the world.

The types of companies regulated in Hong Kong are Limited Liability Companies, Unlimited Liability Companies, Companies Limited by Guarantee, Companies Limited by Shares and General Partners. The type of company preferred for international transactions is the Company Limited by Shares. No minimum capital is required to form a company but a minimum of two directors and two shareholders is required however, they do not need to be residents.

Businesses in this jurisdiction, are able to operate free from government interference and under a simple and low tax regime. Hong Kong offers a commercially advanced environment in which taxes can be considerably minimized, and in several cases completely eliminated. This is an excellent choice for offshore investments.

IRELAND

Ireland is located to the west of Britain, separated by the Irish Sea. The capital and commercial center is Dublin. The official language is English and the official currency is the Irish pound. The legal system is similar to that of Britain, common law. Ireland is divided into the Republic of Ireland and Northern Ireland. The Republic of Ireland is an independent territory. Northern Ireland remains under British rule. The Government of the Republic of Ireland is a parliamentary democracy.

In the past, the Republic of Ireland has traditionally enjoyed a stable political environment despite the constant upheaval with Britain regarding Northern Ireland. It became a member of the European Union in 1973. Its major trading partners are Britain, Germany, France and the U.S. Moreover, in recent years this country has developed a reputation as a banking and money market center. Financing institutions are very strong and sophisticated. Therefore, the handling of trade documents is fast and efficient, and lending facilities are abundant. Also, there are no exchange controls or other financial restraints imposed upon an offshore company.

Even though there is no specific legislation that gives confidentiality to individuals owning a company, there is a common law duty to maintain confidence with respect to all client information.

Through its attractive laws, Ireland encourages foreign companies to do international business on the island. In Ireland, foreign trusts are granted exemption from taxation. As a consequence, a large number of U.S. and European corporations have selected this jurisdiction as their first choice for doing business.

ISLE OF MAN

The Isle of Man is located in the Irish Sea between Britain, Scotland and Ireland. The official language is English and the official currency is the pound Sterling. It is a democratic self-governing territory within the British Commonwealth. Although this island has never formally been a part of Britain, today Britain is responsible for the island's defense and its international relations.

The political, governmental and economic systems are stable and it has a free trade zone. The Isle of Man enjoys a reputation as a respected, well-established and sophisticated offshore financial center. The banking system is well-developed. Confidentiality is very important regarding banking practices. Bankers are not allowed to divulge information related to their clients. Moreover, there are no exchange control regulations of any type to limit the movement of funds on or off the Island, currency is freely transferable.

Non-residents doing business on the island, are exempt from income tax, also it is exempt for trusts with non-residents beneficiaries. There are no capital gains taxes nor gift taxes on the island.

Since this country has a legal system based on Common Law it recognizes the concept of the Trust. The only trust that needs to be registered would be one dealing in real estate. Furthermore, a valid executed trust cannot be revoked. Once it is valid the settlor no longer maintains an interest in the trust property, unless it is provided for in the trust deed. The Isle of Man is an excellent jurisdiction for creative planning and ventures.

JERSEY

The Isle of Jersey is the most southerly of the Channel Islands. It is located 100 miles south of Britain and only 14 miles from the coast of France. The native and official language is English and the currency is the Pound Sterling. It is politically established and the government is a self-governing British dependency with a parliamentary democracy.

The legal system is based on Norman French Customary law, supplemented by legislation and judicial precedent. The economy is based principally on finance, tourism, and agriculture. It has very close links with Britain and the European Union. It is well-regulated, offers confidentiality, and has a highly sophisticated infrastructure. It is also recognized as an international finance center. Its offshore specialties are banking collective investment funds, trust, company administration, and insurance.

A non-resident is only subject to income tax on income originating on the island. A company owned by a non-resident or a trust of which the beneficiaries are non-resident can obtain similar tax treatment. Also, there are no capital, gains, gift, inheritance or general purchase taxes.

It maintains its reputation by ensuring that any new banking institutions which are permitted to establish branches or subsidiaries on the island are of international stature and reputation. Furthermore, confidentiality is a duty for bankers. There are no exchange controls or other financial restraints imposed upon companies. Money in any currency is able to flow into and out of the Island.

The banking industry on this island is well-established and enjoys an international reputation.

LIECHTENSTEIN

The Principality of Liechtenstein is located in central Europe between Austria and Switzerland. The official language is German but most people also speak English and French, and the official currency is the Swiss Franc. The type of government is a male line monarchy on a democratic and parliamentary basis. However, government power is shared by the Prince and the people. In the last forty years this country has experienced an amazing development. It passed from being an agrarian country to one of the world's most highly industrialized nations.

Liechtenstein is attractive to foreign investors who want to operate a company with excellent geographical location, political, economic and social stability, sophisticated and high standard banking, strict bank secrecy, flexible company law, fiscal privileges for domiciliary, absolute anonymity for investors and no tax treaties with other countries involving disclosure of information. Liechtenstein's social and economic infrastructure is very similar to that of Switzerland on both a personal and state level. Its legal system is based on civil law with some common law institutes

As a consequence, it offers a particular combination of both type of laws institutes (type of corporate vehicles): Trust Enterprises and Massachusetts Business Trust for estate planning and commercial purposes, also the classical companies with limited liability and companies limited by shares, and the classical estate planning institutes of foundations and Trust Settlements.

Liechtenstein is one of the most advantageous countries for foreign investors.

LUXEMBOURG

Luxembourg is located in central Europe. Its direct neighbors are Belgium to the northwest, Germany to the east and France to the south. Although the official language is French, German and English are also widely spoken. The official currency is the Luxembourg franc. The legal system is influenced by the German, Belgian and French judicial customs and laws. The government is a hereditary constitutional monarchy and it enjoys political stability. It is a member of the European Community.

The economy is very strong and well-established and the principal industries are iron and steel. Luxembourg has favorable tax and banking laws, which makes this jurisdiction very attractive to offshore investors. This includes financial assistance, tax reductions and credit facilities. Moreover, this country is known as one of the most reputable offshore banking centers in the world. It has a specific secrecy law and violations are considered a civil offense. There are no exchange controls or other financial restraints imposed upon a company. In addition, profits from dividends, interest and other earnings can be freely transferred to other countries.

This jurisdiction has tax treaties avoiding double taxation with a long list of countries including the United States and there are no withholding taxes (imposed on dividends paid by or to an offshore company) or capital gains tax (on the transfer of shares by an offshore company).

Luxembourg also has a free trade zone that cuts across the boundaries of Luxembourg, France and Belgium. This is a choice European jurisdiction for offshore investments.

MADEIRA

Madeira is an island located in the Atlantic Ocean, southwest of Europe. It is part of the territory of Portugal, and therefore a member of the European Union. The official language is Portuguese however, English is widely spoken. The official currency is the Portuguese Escudo. The legal system is based on Civil Law. Even though it is subject to Portuguese authority and law, especially for international matters, it is an autonomous territory with its own regional government and some local regulations. It enjoys political stability and has a strong and stable economy, which is based principally in tourism, the wine industry and agricultural products. This jurisdiction is considered an international financial center. Its main specialties are international services, International shipping register and an industrial free trade zone. There are numerous international banks operating in Madeira, as well as Portuguese banks. Strict secrecy law has to be followed by bankers. There are no exchange controls or other financial restraints imposed upon a company.

Madeira provides numerous tax benefits. There are no corporation, capital gains, property transfer, investment income or withholding taxes and there is no stamp duty. In addition, companies are totally exempt from tax on income generated from activities carried on outside Portugal until the end of the year 2011.

Madeira's strong economy and stable government make this a good choice for offshore businesses.

MALTA

Malta is a group of islands located in the western Mediterranean between Gibraltar and Suez, 60 miles south of Italy. The official languages are English and Maltese, also Italian and French are widely spoken. The official currency is the Maltese lira. The legal system is a mixture of Roman law, Napoleonic Code and English statute law. It is an independent European nation, with a democratic parliamentary system based on the British model. The economy, which is very strong, is principally based on the tourist industry.

Malta is a reputable International financial center and the banking system is very well-developed. A large number of recognized international banks have subsidiaries and branches in the country. It provides very strict rules regarding bank secrecy and confidentiality to the clients. There are no exchange controls or other financial restraints imposed upon a company. Moreover, non-residents are able to freely transfer dividends, royalty income, interest and other payments. Capital can be repatriated with no restrictions.

The type of companies preferred for international transactions are non-trading companies or international trading companies. All companies must have shares representing the capital invested. Shareholder's annual meetings are required however they can be held anywhere in the world. A Registered Office in Malta is necessary however, a Registered Agent is not.

This jurisdiction would be very convenient for international investors, since it offers a lot of different types of incentives. In addition, it enjoys a very good location and it has a well-developed communications system.

MAURITIUS

Mauritius is located in the Indian Ocean, east of Africa English and French are the official languages, and the Mauritian Rupee is the official currency. Before it became an independent nation, it was ruled by Britain. The legal system is based on British and French laws. It has a Westminster type of democracy. It is one of the most politically stable countries in Africa. The economy is also very stable with a free enterprise system and it is based on tourism, financial services (especially offshore), agriculture and manufacturing. It was one of the first Commonwealth countries to get an associate membership in the European Common Market.

Various international banks are currently doing business in Mauritius. Strict bank secrecy must be provided by bankers to their clients. There are no exchange controls, free repatriation of profits and exemption from stamp duties on documents relating to offshore business transactions.

Trust are regulated by Mauritius' legislation. The Offshore Trust is the ideal vehicle for offshore investors. This is a trust in which the settlor is not able to be a resident (at any time in the duration of the trust), however, at least one trustee needs to be a resident. It is exempt from any kind of tax and all filling requirement. The trust is considered irrevocable unless it is expressed otherwise in the trust document. Formation of "asset protection trusts" is permitted. In this case the transfer of trust property to the trustees cannot be voided by the settlor's bankruptcy or liquidation. A stable economy and strong free enterprise system make this a desirable location.

NEVIS AND ST. KITTS

Nevis and St. Kitts are two islands located in the eastern Caribbean. Both islands comprise a single sovereign nation. Before 1983, their political status was that of a British colony. The official language is English and the official currency is the Eastern Caribbean dollar. Its legal system is based on English common law. The government is a constitutional monarchy with Westminster-style parliament. Queen Elizabeth II is the head of the state, and is represented by a Governor-General, who acts on the advice of the prime minister and the cabinet. It is a member of the British Commonwealth, the United Nations, the Organization of Eastern Caribbean States, The Caribbean Community and the Common Market (CARICOM).

The economy of Nevis and St. Kitts has experienced strong growth over the past five years and is very stable. It is based on tourism, agriculture (sugar production), light manufacturing and financial services. The banking system is well-developed and the reputation of their international banks is well known. Confidentiality and bank secrecy are imposed by law.

Tax exemption privileges are provided to companies, limited partnerships and trusts which conduct their business exclusively with individuals who are non-residents. Those tax exemption privileges include: corporate tax, trustee tax status, personal income tax, withholding tax, capital gains tax, gift tax, sales tax, turnover tax or estate duty. Furthermore, there are no exchange controls or other financial restraints applicable to offshore businesses. Strong growth and a stable economy makes this jurisdiction another favorite.

PANAMA

The Republic of Panama has a very interesting and advantageous location, especially for commerce purposes. The Canal makes this country one of the most sophisticated trade zones in the world. It joins South and Central America. Its neighbors are Costa Rica to the west and Colombia to the east. The official language is Spanish, but English is the commonly used second language. It has a democratic government with an elected President.

The major industries are banking, shipping and agriculture, and the major trading partners are the U.S., Germany and Costa Rica.

Since Panama offers tax freedom for international transactions, many international investors have chosen this jurisdiction to do business. This country does not assess any income tax on income produced by offshore sources. Panama offers other incentives as well, such as investment incentives, especially for industries that produce manufactured goods.

Panama has a well-developed and largely recognized banking and foreign exchange center. In fact, the banking system has increased enormously in the last few years, over one hundred commercial banks offer domestic and offshore services in the country. Moreover, the medium of exchange is the U.S. dollar. There are no exchange restrictions or other financial restraints imposed upon a company.

Panama is an advantageous country for trust operations. There is a special tax treatment regarding trusts, in which income on property and on transfer of assets is exempt from taxation where a resident trust has offshore source income or offshore situs assets.

SEYCHELLES

The Seychelles is composed of a group of over 100 islands, located in the southwestern part of the Indian Ocean. The capital is the city of Victoria, which is located on the principal island of Mahe. The official languages are French and English and Creole is widely spoken as well. The official currency is the Seychelles rupee. The legal system is based on both English Common law and French Civil law (Napoleonic Code). It is an independent nation within the Commonwealth and its political status is very stable. The government is a multi-party democracy.

The economy was initially based on the tourism industry however, the financial sector is growing very fast and it makes a considerable contribution to the economy.

The banking system is recognized and well-developed, and it is regulated by the Financial Institutions Act. This Act places the Central Bank as the financial supervisor of offshore banking and other financial transactions. There are numerous international banks and financial companies doing business in the Seychelles.

Trusts can easily be formed and are regulated by modern legislation. An international trust can be used either to hold shares or to achieve a special business purpose by carrying on business without an intermediate company, or to safeguards assets from future creditors. The trustee has to be a resident.

This is a jurisdiction with unlimited advantages for international investors. Furthermore, it is not only a great place to do business, but also to vacation.

SINGAPORE

Singapore is an island located to the south east of Asia. Its neighbors are Malaysia to the west and Indonesia to the north. The native languages are Malay, English and Mandarin and the official currency is the Singapore dollar. It used to be a British Colony in the nineteenth century, but today it is an independent republic with a democratic government. The head of state is an elected president and it enjoys a great deal of political stability. Its legal system is based on English Common Law and it is a member of the Federation of Malaysia.

In recent years its economic growth has been one of the highest in the world. The economy is based primarily on financial and business services. It has a free trade zone and it functions as a free port serving Southeast Asia, North America and Europe.

This jurisdiction is considered one of the major banking centers of the Southeast Asia region. The banking industry was first established on the island in 1840. It offers various advantages as one of the largest financial centers in the world. As a consequence, a considerable number of multi-national companies have concentrated their attention on this country. Some of its offshore specialties are international holding companies, captive insurance, and fund management.

Singapore does not tax interest on bank deposits earned by non-residents, nor income earned by non-residents investing offshore funds outside the country (no withholding tax). Furthermore, there are no exchange controls.

This is an excellent jurisdiction for foreign investors, since Singapore's government is always encouraging international investments.

SWITZERLAND

Switzerland is located in the heart of Europe. It is bordered by Austria, Germany and Italy. Although it is small country, many languages are spoken including German, French and Italian. It has a stable government known for its neutrality, a stable currency (with almost no restrictions), and low interest rates. Switzerland's economy is divided into four sectors: agriculture, manufacturing, handicraft and general services.

Switzerland is considered the world leader in private banking Therefore, it may be one of the best places for location of assets. Swiss banks consider themselves universal banks. Almost without any restrictions, a licensed Swiss bank can have numerous banking activities such as commercial or personal credits, deposits, mortgage lending, asset management, and investment banking.

Swiss banks are acknowledged internationally for the level of safeguards with respect to private wealth, mainly because of the bank secrecy law and the duty of confidentiality. This Swiss law says that the employee or agent of a Swiss bank has a statutory and a contractual duty to keep all the client's information confidential, including information about customers and third parties. Any breach of this confidentiality duty exposes the bank and its employees to a claim for damages. This well-recognized country is ideal for international investors.

TURKS AND CAICOS ISLANDS

The Turks and Caicos Islands consist of two island groups separated by a 22 mile-wide passage. They are located in the Caribbean Sea, 575 miles south east part of Florida and north of Haiti and the Dominican Republic. The official language is English and the official currency is the US dollar. It is a British dependent territory and Britain is responsible for internal security, external affairs and defense. Furthermore, Britain provides financial aid to the Islands. The legal system is based on British Common Law with some local modifications. It has a measure of self-government (a Governor representing the Queen) and it enjoys political and social stability.

The Turks and Caicos have a very stable economy based on tourism and international financial services, followed by the fishing industry. The economy has been continually growing for the past ten years, and it has a free market type of economy. The following taxes do not apply in the Turks and Caicos Islands; income, profit, sales, distributions, capital gains, gifts, inheritance, succession, property, and dividends. This jurisdiction is recognized as an international financial business center. The financial services sector has developed significantly since the creation of the International Company Business (or exempted company). There are several large International banks that have branches and subsidiaries doing business on the Islands.

This excellent location permits easy access to North Central and South America